LIVING POSITIVELY

An exploration into life's joys with applied positive psychology

MSc SAKIS GIOUSSOS

First published in 2019 by Sakis Gioussos

The Positive Academy Ltd
Karola Smidkeho 1819/1
Ostrava - Poruba 70800
Czech Republic.

Written by Sakis Gioussos.

ISBN: 978-80-270-5662-0

www.thepositiveacademy.net

CONTENTS

INTRODUCTION — 5

INNATE AND LEARNED OPTIMISM — 7

50% GENETIC HAPPINESS — 23

MOOD - DOSE (HAPPY NEUROCHEMICALS) — 31

MONEY AND HAPPINESS — 41

BODIES AND POSITIVITY — 57

PERSONALITY (WHO AM I?) — 69

STRENGTHS AND VIRTUES — 81

POSITIVE SELF-IMAGE / PSYCHO-CYBERNETICS — 93

GRATITUDE, SAVORING AND MINDFULNESS — 107

PASSION — 121

THE GOOD LIFE — 129

PERMA — 139

LIFE IS PLEASURE — 151

MOTIVATION — 163

RESILIENCE — 177

MAKING SENSE OF IT ALL — 189

REFERENCES — 191

INTRODUCTION

T his book explores the mechanisms of psychological behavior with practical tools from applied positive psychology. Major theories of motivation, optimism and personality to broaden your knowledge of *"why we do what we do"*. The scientific answers you were always curious about, but never had time to search for, will be revealed in this positive guide towards fulfilment.

Sakis Gioussos has worked in the field of psychology for more than twenty years and is a qualified Applied Positive Coaching psychologist.

With a Bachelor's degree in Psychology and a Master's degree in Applied Positive Psychology, Sakis is on a quest for a scientific understanding of human behaviour.

He was a co-founder of the Harley Street Academy of Psychotherapy, established in 1997. He is trained in practical psychoanalytical methods, and has extensively studied developments in neuro-linguistic and cognitive behavioural programmes which have supplied him with a broader view of the human psyche.

His passion for guiding people to reach personal milestones has led to the publication of this book.

We are all sometimes overwhelmed by choices. But most of us prefer the freedom of having a choice.

Even picking up this book is a choice!

I hope this book will encourage you to become more optimistic.

For reading flow purposes the references are at the end of the book.

INNATE AND LEARNED OPTIMISM

Positive psychology is the scientific study, which focuses on positive change and preventing mental disorders. This principle is based on human strengths that act as buffers against mental illness. Martin Seligman's (1998) positive psychology preventions of mental disorders include becoming a skilled disputer, as in the training program: *Learned Optimism.*

Yes, I hear you… we've all met people who do not have many possessions, are not extremely intelligent, hugely talented, or stunningly attractive, yet most of the time they're cheerful, charming and fun to be around. If you are one of those magnetic bundles of energy, who won the genetic "optimism" lottery, thank your lucky stars.

Innate optimism comes with a moral burden, as it is your duty to spread as much positivity as possible to those around you.

So, what is optimism?
Optimism is a positive, relatively stable characteristic,

where you expect good outcomes for the future in many aspects of your life.

Making positive appraisals of situations and coping with stress, while making the best you can of encounters is the epitome of optimism. Not only do you visualize your optimistic victories but also the causes too.

The idea of "passing it on" is one that resonates with the idea of optimism. It is seen in *"Mirror Neurons."* This is a common occurrence where people mimic other's mood within minutes. Saying that, I once encountered a coach who believed when in a bad or sad mood you should associate yourself with same state minded people.

I guess not all coaching principles are carved in stone.

What do you think?

Remember the last time you attended a business meeting or a social occasion and one individual lit up the place with their positive energy? Or they sucked up all the positivity out of the room?

That was mirror neurons in action!

Many studies on innate or dispositional optimism revealed an approximate 30% heritable factor. Research on parents and their children regarding optimism and a longer life cycle, showed a genetic foundation. However, so far, scientists haven't found a specific gene responsible for optimism. The only published genome-wide study to date on 3,936 individuals failed to identify correlations with optimism and one gene.

It's not 100% someone's fault if they are skeptical of positive thinking and optimism. In a scientific article published in the US National Library of Medicine: *The Neural Basis of Optimism and Pessimism* (Hecht, 2013) multiple factors played a role in one's optimism, including: focus, locus of control, attribution style, optimism bias, self-esteem, body image, persistence, risk taking, mania and depression.

What about optimism bias?
Tali Sharot (2011) believes that the root of optimism is mental time travel. Mental time travel is the ability to move back and forth through time in our mind and to think about a future positive outcome. Just ask someone you know where they see themselves in five years' time.

Some common answers include:
- Professional success
- Financial security
- Good health
- Fulfilling relationships
- Active lifestyle

Most will see their future as positive. When someone has a bad day, that's all it is, a bad day. The optimistic bias works well in keeping many of us striving forward, towards a better day, week, month, or year.

What about having low expectations?

If you don't expect success, finding love, staying healthy, or accomplishing anything meaningful, you won't be disappointed, right?

Sounds good as a theory, but in practice, it is quite wrong! The main reason is that regardless of a successful outcome or not, people with higher expectations generally feel better. The emphasis, like many things in life, is in the *explanation of the event*. Winning an award feels great and if you don't, at least you enjoyed the journey.

But what happens if you get fired or worse?

"What disturbs men's minds is not events but their judgements on events: And so, when we are disturbed, or distressed, let us never lay the blame on others, but on ourselves, on our own judgements.

To accuse others for one's own misfortunes is a sign of want of education;

To accuse oneself shows that one's education has begun;

To accuse neither oneself nor others shows that one's education is complete."–Epictetus.

Whether you have positive illusions about the future or not, optimism has shown clear benefits in the present. Being hopeful relieves our stress levels and improves our physical health by putting our mind at ease. Good expectations reduce anxiety too and optimists are more likely to take vitamins, eat healthily and exercise more often. All these are prerequisites for wellbeing.

The environment also plays a major part in optimism from an early age. Parental modelling in many studies has been the core transmission. It is also possible that optimism can increase through the various strategies, which parents use in their successes.

A sample of 521 families on 11-year-olds in a cross-sectional study concluded that parent optimism leads to child optimism and social competence.

Positive parenting behaviors include:

Warmth, affection, monitoring, and positive engagement as essential factors for optimism growth.

Now let's look at what *learned optimism* is and how we can increase it.

Learned optimism

I am a born pessimist.

What can you do with that? Blame it on your parents, environment, teachers, or experiences?

According to Martin Seligman, one of the founding fathers of positive psychology:

"Our explanatory style of events defines us as either optimists or pessimists."

For example, if you are fired, not an uncommon occurrence, do you perceive this as:

Personal

I am not good enough.
There's something wrong with me.

Permanent

I will never find another job.

Pervasive

I am also a bad parent.

or

Impersonal
The company is struggling.
My skill-set was not needed.

Impermanent
I will soon find a better job.

Specific
This only affects my work and not my family, friends, hobbies and other interests.

Similarly, a simple a-b-c-d-e technique based on Albert Ellis' ABC's 1960s model, can also change our cognitive appraisal patterns. The different point of view can help us look at experiences in a clearer dimension. Seligman states that to an extent the pre-disposed pessimist can increase their optimism by interpreting events differently.

Adversity - Event causing stress.
Belief - How you interpret the event.
Consequence - The resulting action from the belief.
Disputation - Challenge negative thoughts from A to C.
Energizing - Once you condition yourself towards positive thoughts and behaviors, a feeling of good energy can become an often-occurring outcome.

Psychologists call this strategy new habit forming, where instead of catastrophizing about every little thing that does not go your way, you practice a-b-c-d-e.

Another common situation for many is when passing a colleague, or acquaintance and saying hello, and they ignore you.

You could think:
Did I do something wrong?
They don't like me.
They found out something bad about me?

Or you could think:
They might have been in a rush.
They didn't see me, or hear me.
They were day dreaming.

TIP!
One way to handle similar situations is to raise your voice when addressing someone and to make strong eye contact. It's not a bulletproof plan, but I am sure that the probability of a reaction will be higher: *mirror neurons in action.*

Our beliefs of an event and the mental choices and spin we put on it, is still within our power.

IS POSITIVE CHANGE POSSIBLE?
Once upon a time, a boy was born to Greek parents in the late 1960s in Thessaloniki, Greece. From thirty days' old the infant slept with his grandmother, on a foldout couch latching on to her nightgown collar for dear life. This sleeping pattern continued until age eleven, where the boy gave up his

granny's collar to sleep in his own bedroom, in a foreign city (London - England).

During, the first eleven years he was told to keep quiet and not to speak loudly or answer back. After most afternoon naps (still common in south Europe), *the boy used to wake up crying.*

He was so shy he was afraid to ask for anything when visiting other family members' houses, including using the bathroom facilities.

He enjoyed playing with other children though, both outdoor and indoor games, and spent many hours alone, re-arranging his big collection of toy soldiers. You could say that this was an introverted and shy boy with some fear issues, which included sleeping alone.

Fast-forward to age eleven years and three months, the boy's father took him to London. Keep in mind the little Greek boy could not speak a word of English, so the first year was tough. Thanks to his English stepmother who taught him many important life lessons, the boy started to change.

However, the biggest change happened at age twelve, when his dad told him he was too skinny, too short and too weak for life in London. What happened next was the moment everything changed in the young shy boy's life. His dad offered him a whole English pound note if he squatted

*fifteen times while holding a 10kg bag of potatoes. The task
was completed.*

Later that evening, T. J Hooker (a popular cop show) *was
on TV. The boy, now feeling proud of his accomplishment,
pointed to the TV screen and asked his dad "Why wasn't I
born with a body like that"?*

*His dad turned around and said: "Son, you can have that
body if you want, and anything else you might wish for in
life, all you have to do is believe in yourself."*

EPIPHANY

The young boy was me.

I played football every day after school, until the P. E
teacher chose me to play for the school football team.
Several school children now knew my name and cheered
me on during football games. I also gained well wanted
attention from a few girls too.

This positive change sparked a whole raft of other interests
including singing, dancing, acting, karate and even a short-
lived pop band.

Whoever has met me since then would describe me as one
of the most cheerful people they have ever met.

Believe me, change is possible for everyone, I am living

proof. I don't mean that every introvert will become
an extroverted, attention-seeking comedian. But my
change was due to the adventures, environments and
encouragement I was exposed to in London.
Granny Eva suppressed the innate extroverted nature I
was born with during my first eleven years of childhood.
Gradual development in different areas from speaking
more clearly to becoming better at sports can boost one's
general confidence and positivity in life.

Additional benefits of learned optimism

Plenty of evidence shows how becoming more optimistic
is also good for your health. We've all heard about the
dangers of stress and the ailments it causes: heart disease,
asthma attacks, obesity, diabetes, headaches, depression,
anxiety, gastrointestinal problems, and speeding up of
aging to name just a few.

The increase in mental and physical wellbeing, through
learned optimism practices have also helped people achieve
more success in the business world too. In over 600 studies,
Seligman found that optimistic explanations increase your
career and business chances of success:

"Optimists make more money and are more loyal."

Seligman discovered this phenomenon in one of the
toughest sales jobs, that of a life insurance rep.
The research showed that optimistic sales reps sold 88%

more than pessimistic reps. There was also evidence that pessimists on the bottom 25% in sales, were more likely to quit than optimists in the same bottom 25%. Other studies of different occupations showed similar results.

"Optimists move forward due to their belief of options."
-Martin Seligman.

Pessimists rarely persist when faced with setbacks and they remain unchanged.

"What is the point?" they may ask.

"Nothing will change anyway."

They have already made up their minds as to the outcome.

Optimism and living longer
In the 1930s, the National Institute, with a grant from the Kelberg Foundation, conducted one of the most convincing studies of happiness on a group of nuns in Kentucky, USA. The research involved having each nun write an autobiographical sketch upon their acceptance into the convent. Six decades later, the contents of the sketches proved to be strong indicators of whether the author was still alive.

What makes this study so convincing is that by following a group of people with identical life histories, it eliminated all the possible variables, such as differences in diet, or socioeconomic background. Yet despite the nuns' similar habits, some of them experienced long, illness-free lives, while others succumbed to death at an early age.

It turns out that the nuns who had expressed the most positive emotions in their journal entries were the same ones who were still alive and kicking sixty years later.
A full ninety percent of the most cheerful quarter of nuns were still alive at age eighty-five while only thirty-four percent of the least cheerful quarter survived.
The happiest nuns lived a full ten years longer.

One of my favorite quotes from a Charles Swindoll's poem:
"We cannot change our past… we cannot change the fact that people will act in a certain way.
We cannot change the inevitable.
The only thing we can do is play on the one string we have, and that is our attitude…
I am convinced that life is 10% what happens to me and 90% how I react to it… And so, it is with you…
We are in charge, of our attitudes." –Charles Swindoll.

Additional notes

Whether you're born with a high amount of optimism or not, the good news is that optimism can be learned. Our perception of life can become distorted through experiences of hardship.

The happy-go-lucky optimists are easy to spot from a mile away, as they wear a smile on their face and often look on the bright side of life.

For those of you not predisposed with optimism, remember that the way we interpret events can influence our mood, even from the people closest to us.
For example, a couple can watch the same movie together and yet disagree on its meaning. Optimism is a point of view and a choice in more situations than you might think.

THE TWO TRAVELERS

There was once a traveler who was walking from a village in the mountains to a village in the valley.

As he walked along, he saw a monk working in a field, so he stopped and said to the monk, "I'm on my way to the village in the valley, can you tell me what it's like?"

The monk looked up from his labor and asked the man where he had come from. The man replied, "I have come from the village in the mountains."

"What was that like?" the monk asked "Terrible!" the man said. "No one spoke my language, I had to sleep on a dirt floor in one of their houses, they fed me some sort of stew that had yak or dog or both in it and the weather was atrocious."

"Then I think that you will find that the village in the valley is much the same," the monk said. A few hours later another traveler passed by and he said to the monk, "I am on my way to the village in the valley, can you tell what it's like?"

"Where have you come from?" asked the monk. "I have come from the village in the mountains."

"And what was that like?"

"It was awesome!" the man replied, "No one spoke my language, so we had to communicate using our hands and facial expressions. I had to sleep on the dirt floor which was cool as I've never done that before. They fed me some sort of weird stew and I have no idea what was in it but just to experience how the locals lived was great and the weather was freezing cold, which meant that I got a taste of the local conditions. It was one of the best experiences of my life." "Then I think that you'll find that the village in the valley is much the same," responded the monk.

"Positive thinking is the notion that if you think good thoughts, things will work out well. Optimism is the feeling of thinking things will be well and to be hopeful."
-Martin Seligman.

CHAPTER 2

50% GENETIC HAPPINESS

Innate happiness is fifty percent in our genes.

On exploring optimism and positive living, it's necessary to look at the genetic/inherited part of happiness passed down from our biological parents.

Sonja Lyubomirsky's wide research on happiness is the foundation of the famous pie chart, which sets the genetic baseline of happiness at 50%. Lyubomirsky concluded on this pre-dispositional percentage after reviewing the Minnesota, U.S.A twin studies.

Research from Lykken and Tellegen (1996), found well-being correlation levels of 50% in fraternal twins sharing 100% same genes. The non-identical twins showed a variation of 2-8%. The key aspect from the percentage, is that it's possible to change our current levels of happiness.

But why be happy in the first place?

Social rewards

Abundance of friends

Fulfilling social interactions

Lasting marriage probability

Job benefits

Higher income

More creativity

More energy

Personal benefits

Longer life

Healthier immune system

Better coping strategies

10% life circumstance happiness

Our life circumstances, which include being married, single, educated, rich, attractive, etc. account approximately for only 10% of our current level of happiness. That's because of something positive psychologists call the *hedonic treadmill.*

For instance, say you:
- Buy a new car.
- Build a new house.
- Start a new relationship.
- Get a new job.

How long do you think that first elevation of happiness

you experienced at the beginning will last? As many of you have experienced by now and an abundance of studies show, not very long!

40% intentional activity happiness
Intentional activities induce the 40% at our disposal, which requires continuous practice.

Behavioral activities – exercise, kindness, intimacy, socializing, etc.

Cognitive activities – gratitude, positive thinking, optimism, etc.

Volitional/Will activities – goal setting, finding purpose, etc.

The impermanent nature of intentional activity acts as a shield and preventive measure towards hedonic treadmill adaptation. Other intentional activities that have been shown to increase happiness include:

- Getting a good night's sleep.
- Setting achievable goals (SMART).
- Taking a break and reflecting on the positives (gratitude).
- Sexual intimacy.
- Moving away from the money equals happiness myth.
- Building close relationships.

- Savoring (being present in the pleasant experience).
- Physical activity (exercise of any kind).
- Taking part in flow experiences (when you lose track of time during an activity).

Please keep in mind that happiness is a subjective and fleeting feeling, making it a nice by-product of doing things we enjoy.

The happiness pie chart does not define the exact percentages in everyone, but the generic definitions of temperaments (Galen, 160 A.D) are still used.

A *sanguine* person is easy to spot just as is a *choleric*.

Phlegmatic people need time to think things through.

Melancholic temperaments need to step out a little.

Optimism and spontaneity are naturally higher in some temperaments than others. However, the goal is *one*, and that is to enjoy more of life's fruits and blessings.

> *"When we are happy—when our mind-set and mood are positive, we are smarter, more motivated, and thus more successful. Happiness is the center, and success revolves around it."* -Shawn Achor.

On success, many studies have shown that happiness equals success and not vice versa.

"Success is not the key to happiness. Happiness is the key to success. If you love what you are doing, you will be successful." -Albert Schweitzer.

If people are incentivized, and in a perfect environment, they will be happy and that will show both in their professional and personal lives.

"Happy people are more likeable and more sociable. They are also better able to cope with stress and likely to be healthier and live longer." -Sonja Lyubomirsky.

Additional notes

Studies have shown that our birth temperament is only part of what makes a happy person. The good news shown in multiple research is that the happiness factor is one which we have control over. So, what if others have a head start?

In the big scheme of things, it doesn't matter that much, as the intentional activities we take part in have more effect on our general happiness.

I've heard people say, many times, I will be happy when:
- I get the promotion.
- Buy my dream house.
- Marry the boy/girl of my dreams.

- Start a family.
- Graduate from university.
- And so on....

As most of us have found out by now, once we have fulfilled our initial wishes, our psyche will look for the next challenge. So, avoid the hedonic treadmill by taking- action to bring happiness into your life with small intentional activities.

The journey is the most important part in reaching any goal as once the goal is reached we take it for granted.

FINDING HAPPINESS

Once a group of fifty people were attending a seminar. During a group activity, the seminar leader gave each attendee one balloon on which each person was asked to write their name with a marker pen. Then all the balloons were collected and put in another room.

The delegates were taken into that room and asked to find the balloon which had their name written on within five minutes.

Everyone was frantically searching for their name, colliding with each other, pushing around others and there was utter chaos.

At the end of five minutes no one could find their own balloon. Now each one was asked to randomly collect a balloon and give it to the person whose name was written on it. Within minutes everyone had their own balloon.

The speaker then said, "This is happening in our lives. Everyone is frantically looking for happiness all around, not knowing where it is. Our happiness lies in the happiness of other people. Give them their happiness; you will get your own happiness. And this is the purpose of human life... the pursuit of happiness."

CHAPTER 3

MOOD – DOSE (HAPPY NEUROCHEMICALS)

Some 2,400 years ago the Greek physician Hippocrates (460–370 BCE) introduced the four humors: *yellow bile, black bile, blood and phlegm.* This was the first connection between mind and body. The modern era of innovative technologies (MRI - PET scans, etc.) dismissed the four humors theory when a reward center was discovered in the human brain.

In the 1960s, neuroscientific focus investigated emotional experience and its connection to electrochemical reactions in the brain. Science deemed the nerve cells as responsible for inducing neurochemicals in the control center *(nucleus accumbens).*

The nucleus accumbens, or the pleasure and reward system (in the middle of the brain) manages many characteristics including feelings of love, happiness, laughter and euphoria.

Imbalances have known to cause obsessive compulsive disorder, bipolar disorder and anxiety disorder. The VTA *(ventral tegmental area),* another group of neurons close to the nucleus accumbens, handles pleasurable sensations.

Without getting too scientific, the four primary neurochemicals in the human brain that effect our mood and levels of happiness are:

Dopamine–Oxytocin–Serotonin–Endorphins = DOSE. So, let's start with dopamine.

Dopamine (Motivation - Reward molecule)
There are around eighty-six billion neurons in our brain and they communicate with each other via brain chemicals called neurotransmitters. Dopamine is the neurotransmitter, which relates most to the sensation of pleasure and the motivation to seek that pleasure. It is one of the most studied neurotransmitters, not just because it gives us a zest for life, but for the addictions it gives us too. Dopamine is our motivation molecule, as it boosts our drive, concentration, goal setting and resistance to impulses. It is produced in several areas of the brain including the *substantia nigra* and *ventral tegmental area (VTA).* Low levels of dopamine can lead to feeling lethargic, mood swings, memory loss, hopelessness, apathy, procrastination and sleeping problems.

Two ways to increase dopamine

Unhealthy way

Large amounts of caffeine, alcohol, sugar, drugs, shopping, promiscuous unprotected sex, video games, online-porn and gambling. These are all temporary dopamine boosters that can all become self-destructing and addictive behaviors.

Healthy way

Diet: eating foods like apples, almonds, bananas, beans, peanuts, watermelon to name just a few. Apart from vitamins and supplements, a healthy lifestyle can also increase dopamine levels. Proven ways for getting the most out of dopamine include: exercise, meditation, music, massages and a good night's sleep. Dopamine is mainly increased by setting small goals and achieving them regularly.

Oxytocin (Bonding molecule)

People also know oxytocin as the "love hormone" or "hug drug". It increases feelings of trust and empathy, which leads to stronger bonds. The hypothalamus (in the center of our brain) creates oxytocin, and the word comes from the Greek words "oxys" (quick) and "tokos" (birth). Oxytocin occurs during childbirth in all mammals.

Higher levels of oxytocin are released by both sexes during orgasm and women experience it during breastfeeding.

Loyalty, trust, generosity, warmth, and being sociable and extroverted has roots in higher levels of oxytocin.

Lack of oxytocin

Symptoms of little oxytocin include anger, fear, anxiety, lack of enjoyment in social interactions and affection.

How to increase oxytocin

Even though some cultures might find touching inappropriate, it's called the *hug drug* for a reason. Hugs, petting animals, long baths, giving gifts, switching off electronic devices when communicating with others and giving them your full attention, sharing your meal and staying in touch with your loved ones are good ways to boost oxytocin levels.

Studies in people taking part in adrenaline-boosting activities, such as roller coaster rides and sky-dives, showed a 200% increase in oxytocin levels. Let me be clear in saying that this is not for everyone and please seek medical advice before taking part in high risk adrenaline activities.

Caution

Too much oxytocin is not healthy, as it can make people feel over-protective of their own tribe, race, identity, colleagues and even sports team. The neuroscientist Simone Shamay – Tsoory and her colleagues (2009) conducted a study in Israel on fifty-six volunteers who were given oxytocin through a nasal inhaler. During the experiment the participants showed aggression, an inclination to lie, envy, gloat and xenophobia.

However, these negative side-effects, were only seen in participants who inhaled artificial oxytocin. So, it wouldn't be fair to blame oxytocin alone for feelings of jealousy and aggression.

Serotonin (confidence molecule)

Serotonin is a neurotransmitter involved in regulating mood, feelings of relaxation, sleep, and appetite. When levels of this neurotransmitter are high in the brain, we feel happy, calm, and balanced. Researchers link low levels of serotonin to anxious thoughts, irritable moods, and restlessness.

Brain - stomach link

Serotonin is also known as the second brain as it is found in our digestive system. It is estimated that up to ninety per-cent of this natural feel good drug is produced by microbes in our intestines. The rest is found in the brain and the central nervous system. Many of our emotions are most likely influenced by the nerves in our gut.

Butterflies in the stomach when excited, or nervousness is a sign of a physiological stress response. Most antidepressant medications use the selective serotonin reuptake inhibitors (*SSRIS*), which increase serotonin levels.

Some other benefits related to a healthy amount of serotonin include:

- Good bowel movements
- Stimulation of quality sleep
- Faster wound healing
- Increased libido
- Healthy skin
- Weight loss
- Brain maturation
- Relief of stress and anxiety

Natural boost of serotonin levels

Nutrition – eggs, cheese, pineapples, salmon, turkey, nuts and seeds. Eating healthily can prevent sugar spikes and crashes caused by high carb and sugary foods. Fast foods are the worst, so limitation is essential.

Exercise – along with movement, exercise is the single best method of balancing neurotransmitters. One of the main reasons is the natural boost of *tryptophan*, which occurs after exercise and is the main building block of serotonin.

Artificial light – light therapy is a well-known treatment for seasonal affective disorder. It is also effective at other times too. White light sessions provide better results in the morning.

Sunlight – vitamin D is good for our bones, can prevent the onset of depression, and strengthen our immune system.

Positive thoughts – Positron Emission Tomography (PET) scans measured people in positive and negative moods.

Studies found higher serotonin levels in those with positive moods.

Priming – is a nonconscious technique where you can stimulate associations. For example, someone who sees the word yellow can faster recognize the word banana. Psychotherapists use priming to train a person's memory in positive ways.

Endorphins (pain killing molecule)
Endorphins are natural opiate painkillers and are manufactured by the central nervous system (brain, spinal cord) and pituitary gland. That amazing feeling after a good workout, or a runner's high is the result of an increase in endorphins.

Endorphins are released in response to stress, but also during sex or eating. Endorphins have also shown to help social attachment as humans are naturally inclined to seek pleasure and avoid pain.

Symptoms of a lack of endorphins
There is a high probability that when low in endorphins the following experiences might occur: mood swings, aching and pain, anxiety, depression, impulsive behavior, sleeping problems.

Extra benefits of endorphins
- Self-esteem and optimism

- Reduced stress and anxiety
- Weight reduction
- Confidence

How to increase endorphins

Multiple natural ways include: laughter, sex, exercise, dark chocolate, dance, artistic creation, a massage, a sauna, a favorite food, a favorite show, music and spicy food.

Neuroscientists are not sure of the reason why some prescriptive medicine targeting certain neurotransmitters work better on some people than others.

The one thing that highly correlates to happiness and well-being is lifestyle. By developing healthy practices, you will find an overlap in boosting all the four happy neurochemicals.

Additional notes

The take-home message is to lead a healthy lifestyle. Gaining and sustaining a good mood is not rocket-science. The practical steps are a start, but the most important thing is to listen to your body.

Many ailments can be avoided by choosing the healthier and common-sense option. It's not necessary to become a health guru to stabilize a good mood. Tap into your instincts and pleasant memories and pursue those interests. Fluctuating mood is normal, provided you are in a good mood more often than in a bad mood. The most qualified person to control your mood swings with your natural neurochemicals is you.

BALL SIZE

After a two-year study, the National Science Foundation concluded the following regarding America's ball-related recreational preferences:

The sport of choice for unemployed or incarcerate people is **basketball**.

The sport of choice for maintenance level employees is **bowling.**

The sport of choice for blue-collar workers is **football.**

The sport of choice for supervisors is **baseball.**

The sport of choice for middle management is **tennis.**

The sport of choice for corporate officers is **golf.**

Conclusion: *The higher you rise in the corporate structure, the smaller your balls become.*

I hope this short story enhanced your good mood☺.

CHAPTER 4

MONEY AND HAPPINESS

In materialistic terms, Marcus Aurelius might have been right in saying that, *"a man's worth is no greater than the worth of his ambitions."* But perhaps he overlooked the fact that a man's worth does not equal his well-being.

The Beatles sang *"money can't buy you love"*.

But can money buy you happiness?

And if it did, how much would it take?

When does money, stop making you feel good?

Does more money and recognition = more happiness?

For those of you who think riches are the answer…

"I hope everybody could get rich and famous and will have everything they ever dreamed of, so they will know that it's not the answer." –Jim Carrey.

I am realistic when addressing money. There are many global studies on money and happiness which point towards an *ideal monetary number.*

The current global ideal yearly salary, or cap in where more money makes little or no difference in your levels of happiness as of 2018:

 $60,000 to $75,000 per year, per person, per household, (two adults $150,000) for emotional well-being *(day-to-day feelings of anger, sadness, happiness, excitement etc.).*

$95,000 per year, per person, per household, (two adults $190,000) for life satisfaction *(cognitive assessment of how you are generally doing).*

I am reluctant to agree that the afore-mentioned numbers are a global monetary norm. I can think of quite a few developed countries where the average yearly salaries are much lower.

Research showed that in North America the figure for life satisfaction was even higher at:

$65,000 to $95,000 per year, per person, per household (two adults $190,000) for well-being.

$105,000 per year, per person, per household (two adults $210,000) for life satisfaction.

Current global money studies leave a lot to be desired. An internet search will show the differences in the wealthy lifestyles of the Manhattan, New York elite compared to the high earners in Budapest, Hungary.

However, the studies also showed that after reaching these levels of income, no further benefits were shown in life satisfaction, or emotional well-being.

Research on lottery winners also showed a cap on money and satisfaction. After the initial burst of immediate happiness, in the long-term the new millionaires on average were no more happy than ordinary people.

Freedom - work-life balance
"No people can be happy if they do not feel they are choosing the course of their own life." -Meik Wiking.

In the *"Little Book of Lykke"*, Wiking explores his own Danish heritage and writes about capitalistic working hours: The average annual hours worked per worker is 1,457 in Denmark, compared to 1,674 in the UK, and 1,790 in the US.

Denmark = 182 working days a year.

UK = 210 working days a year.

US = 224 working days a year.

So, are we becoming capitalist westerners?

Are we turning into slaves of our own desires? Drooling over the latest shiny gadget that we will soon grow bored of?

"We spend money we don't have, to buy things we don't need, to impress people we don't like." –Dave Ramsey.

Greece

I believe the currently financially burdened citizens of Greece learned that lesson too well. The times of wearing 350 Euro sunglasses, driving expensive German cars, wearing Italian designer clothes and partying every other night until sunrise, are a distant memory for many.

Greece is a country that depends on tourism, as it boasts some of the best beaches, tastiest food and oldest civilizations on earth. It saddens me to think of this culture with a rich history that introduced to much of the western world: philosophy, education, music, poetry, mathematics, medicine, engineering, history, astronomy, mythology etc. at the mercy of the world's financial institutions and asking for a monetary bailout.

Country happiness

First, I would like to address the money happiness issue, at a country/state level, before we look at individual happiness.

Positive psychology approaches this topic by consulting the Word Happiness Report (a survey which is annually updated with a participation of 155 countries). As of 2017, Norway tops the global happiness rankings followed by Denmark (a previous winner), Iceland, Switzerland, Finland, Netherlands, Canada, New Zealand, Australia with Sweden making it to number ten on the list.
Now at first glance, the top ten countries have a rather high average income. However, if we search a little further, the accountable factors are based on six key variables, of which one is income:

- Income
- Healthy life expectancy
- Having someone to count on in times of trouble
- Generosity
- Freedom
- Trust in business transactions and government.

Aside from the obvious GDP (gross domestic product) and other five key variables, the main finding was that 80% of the variance in happiness occurred within countries.

Social issues such as mental health, physical health and relationships were an important factor. However, income inequality and mental illness was influential in poorer countries.

This is shown at the bottom of the World Happiness Report where the unhappiest ten countries were: Yemen, South Sudan, Liberia, Guinea, Togo, Rwanda, Syria, Tanzania, Burundi and Central African Republic sitting last at number 155.

My Greek compatriots sit at number eighty-seven.

My fellow-Brits with their frequent weather complaints are nineteenth.

However, my current compatriots, the Czechs, who are well known for their pessimism and xenophobia made it to number twenty-three in 2017. (Things are positively changing).

China, one of the fastest growing economies of the last twenty-five years, has seen their happiness level drop back to their 1990 level, sitting at seventy-ninth place.

As for the U.S.A, their reduced levels of happiness, regardless of their wealth growth, has them placed fourteenth, a huge drop from third place back in 2007.

So, apart from all of us migrating to the top ten happiest countries in the world, half of which are Nordic, what else have the money and happiness studies shown us?

In the *"Myths of Happiness"* Sonja Lyubomirsky explains

that there is a correlation between money and happiness, but *not a strong one.*

Common sense tells us that more money can give us greater health care, more autonomy, financial freedom, security and a good education to name just a few.

Who doesn't want to live in a safe neighborhood, or have the resourses and freedom to travel? How about being able to cope with some of life's hardships like job loss or marriage breakups?

This is where it gets interesting.

When wealthy people are asked about their general level of happiness, monetary advantages push their satisfaction levels higher than the average or low earners.

However, when richer people are asked to rate their feelings of moment to moment happiness during their daily lives e.g. how joyful, affectionate, grateful, or sad, angry etc. they are, their positive emotions are not higher than those with less money.

This shows that the money equals happiness connection might be a cognitive one in the sense that:

"I have more money, so I should be happier overall."

But money has a much smaller importance on our daily feelings, or to put it simply, our lives.

Some studies have shown that not only can money buy happiness, but happiness can buy money.

This is due to happier people being more proactive in searching for jobs that suit them. Enjoying what you do makes you more proficient, productive, and this rewards you with more money.

A bold statement backed up by a study of thousands of siblings showed that:

"The happier sibling would make more money later in life."

Psychologists base this assumption on the principle that positive people seem more likely to get a degree, find a job, and get promoted.

The study's results are robust and include controls such as education, IQ, physical health, height, self-esteem, and later happiness.

However, the link between money and happiness is stronger for poorer people. Not being able to provide a safe environment and basic needs for yourself, or loved ones detrimentally influences happiness levels.

Research has shown that the cut-off point to how much happier you will be with more money is valid. I guess it might all depend on the subjective view of having adequate income to cover your needs and aspirations.

So, do ambition or aspiration matter?

Ambition and drive are only healthy sometimes!

For the ambitious among us, once we reach our goal we soon plan another to pursue.

Psychologists call this the hedonic treadmill.

We continuously raise the bar for what we want, or feel we need, in-order to be happy - and the hedonic treadmill spins faster with ambition.

The downside to being highly ambitious is a constant sense of dissatisfaction with our current achievements.

As a positive psychologist, I like to separate *ambition* and *aspiration* into two different entities:

Ambition - Innate, trait, disposition, continuous persistence, constantly planning new goals, need for achievement or distinction; sometimes too much can prove negative in the form of greed.

Aspiration - Particular-goal, or object.
Ambition in the Western society individualistic model is seen, as a good thing. However, this is not the case in the traditional Eastern model of collectivism.

Two types of ambition

Healthy ambition: as defined by Aristotle is understood as striving for achievement (life enhancing).

Unhealthy ambition: is striving for achievement using unethical methods, which are destructive and can lead to greed.

Ambition is a mixture of nature and nurture where constant ethical cultivation is necessary for achievement. The trick is to be ambitious while living in the present!

Let us look at a hypothetical monetary scenario:

In dimension A, you make £50,000 per year and everybody else makes £25,000. In dimension B, you make £100,000 per year (so twice as much as before) and everybody else makes £200,000.

Prices are constant, so goods and property, will cost the same in both dimensions

Which would you choose?

In multiple interpretations of this example around the world, most people chose dimension "A".

The American sociologist Thorstein Veblen (1899), coined the term "conspicuous consumption," which describes the phenomenon of buying luxury goods in-order to publicly display your wealth to attain status.

In today's interconnected (social network obsessed) world, you are likely to see and hear in many countries the expression:

"If you've got it, flaunt it."

Personality and freedom of choice usually play their part in the exhibition of wealth!

Maximizer or Satisficer?

Another common psychological interpretation based on people's decision making is the *maximizer* or *satisficer* personality.

Maximizer – Pursues options for maximum utility. By setting themselves high standards a sense of disappointment is normal when they fail to achieve. Buyer's remorse is also common when purchasing a product, as they continue to over-think their initial decision.

Example: You are looking for a new phone at the best price

with the highest storage capacity, camera pixels, etc. Once you purchase the phone you feel satisfied until you start to doubt whether it was the best deal possible. Your eye catches a new offer, ad, or even a friend's new phone. So, disappointment sets in.

Satisficer – Looks for what they want to gain from a situation and will evaluate their options based on what meets their requirements. The economist Herbert A. Simon (1956) proposed the satisficer concept with the idea being one of rational choice. He combined the words "satisfying and sufficing".

TIP 1!

Bibliotherapy is the art of using books to aid people in solving issues they are facing. This has been around for decades, and the belief in the psychological healing power of books can be traced back to ancient Greece and Egypt.

TIP 2!

It is not about how much money you make, but also what you do with the money you have:

Buy more experiences and memories, not things.

TIP 3!

Pay now, consume later…
If you buy an experience, make sure it is well into the future, so you can look forward to it. This provides the

natural dopamine high we get from the anticipation of something.

We think money will bring lots of happiness for a long time, but instead it brings a little happiness for a short time.

Additional notes
In my experience of working with wealthy people from different countries I found that they all share one common characteristic:

They think money.

On a subconscious level, it's always a priority even if they don't like to exhibit their wealth. A quick Google search shows over 199 million results for "how to get rich." This is a strong indication of people's obsession with making a lot of money.

In most happiness questionnaires, people list relationships as number one with money coming in at a close number two. It seems as if we have taken our health for granted. Money is important, but is it worth losing your health over?

There are many examples of rich and privileged people who are addicted to harmful substances and behaviors. Similarly, others will work themselves till burn out, where only a heart attack, or stroke will stop them in their tracks.

Instead of doing good with our money and enjoying financial freedom, some of us choose to destroy our lives, and the people who care for us.

I am saddened when I read stories about the young, talented and successful people who have lost their way.

If money is a means to an end, why are people not happy when they achieve financial freedom?

I believe what you do for the money you earn is more important than how much you make.

A person who likes what they do does not know the meaning of work stress. Enjoying the journey in whatever endeavor is always more important than the result.

Money can keep you sane just as much as it can make you crazy. It's what you do with it that matters.

MONEY CAN'T BUY HAPPINESS

Once upon a time in a land far away there lived a very rich man. He had many businesses and everything that he touched turned to gold. He was a good man and he helped many people along the way, because he could not stand the sight of anyone suffering. As he grew older he started to feel lonely.

All his life he was so busy, building up his empire, that he forgot to live his life. He now had all these successful businesses, and all the money in the world, but he had no one to share it with.

He did not know where to start, so he hired a team of experts with specific specifications to find him the perfect wife. It was not long before they made up a shortlist. He was terribly excited, so he set up interviews with the best candidates... but *he was disappointed with most of these women. None of them was as perfect as he wanted them to be.*

He soon became very depressed. He was so used to getting everything he wanted, that he could not understand why he couldn't find the right woman. He became so focused on finding the right wife, that he lost focus on the rest of his life. His businesses began to suffer, and he started to lose money.

It wasn't long before he lost all his money and his businesses. He even lost his house and everything that he worked so hard for throughout his lifetime. He had to go live in a shelter. He became a miserable grumpy old man, and died as a lonely, poor man. No one even cared enough to go to his funeral.

"The hardest thing to find in life is happiness – money is only hard to find because it gets wasted trying to find happiness." -Anonymous.

CHAPTER 5

BODIES AND POSITIVITY

Plato, (428-348 BC) believed that cognition and soul were in the brain, making the body a separate entity (dualism).

Aristotle, (384-322 BC) argued that emotions resided in the heart, so body and soul were one (monism).

The 1980s brought theories of multiple intelligences, e.g. "kinesthetic" intelligence in athletes and dancers and logical and abstract thinking in architects.

Since Gardener (1983) introduced the mastery over body theory, desire for grace and beauty in movement, a lot of body image issues have impacted society. (Gardener is not held accountable for body image issues).

The rise in beauty enhancement surgery is indicative of today's plastic fantastic syndrome society:
1.8 million surgical and 15.5 million minimal invasive procedures were performed in the U.S.A. alone in 2016.

Topping the plastic surgical chart in 2016 was:
1. Breast augmentation 290,467
2. Liposuction 235, 237
3. Nose reshaping 223,018
4. Eyelid surgery 209,020
5. Facelifts 131,106

Sounds like a yearning for society to manipulate their birth bodies in trying to look younger, thinner and more attractive.

Body Dysmorphic Disorder (BDD)
A mental disorder known as dysmorphophobia (BDD) is the fixation on imperfection when looking in the mirror which affects 1.7% to 2.4% of the population.

I believe the rise of the picture-perfect human specimens in social networks has led to a higher percentage of dysmorphophobia than in the afore-mentioned figure. BDD is a mental disorder that is equally distributed between men and women and surfaces during adolescence.

The signs and symptoms of BDD vary from fixation on minor scars, acne, facial/body hair, size of breasts, size of nose, muscle size, symmetry, size of body, etc. This can lead to social avoidance, excessive exercise and emotional problems including depression.

Unfortunately, only trained clinicians are likely to diagnose BDD. Professionals usually treat patients with medication and therapy. Successful treatment of the condition requires self-education and a strong discipline, especially in not skipping therapy sessions.

Avoidance of alcohol and drugs and a healthy amount of exercise has also shown to lessen symptoms.

Positive psychology
Holistic perspective:
It would be a daunting task to seek happiness and feel optimistic, without caring about our body's well-being.

Embodiment is the term used in positive psychology when addressing issues of a healthy body/healthy mind.

Psychologists generally describe it as:
a) The awareness of and responsiveness to bodily sensations.
b) Thoughts, feelings and behaviours are grounded in sensory experiences and bodily states.

Interpersonal relationships
Our first line of communication from birth is touch, so embodiment is crucial from day one. Social interactions are affected by coordinated movement and synchrony to attachment and feelings of compassion.

A positive body image in individuals has shown higher levels of psychological and well-being including optimism and self-esteem. Healthier eating habits and a more virile sex life are positive side-effects of feeling good in your body.

So, let's look at what some studies have indicated as being a healthy lifestyle.

Physical activity

We've all heard about the 10,000 step a day rule, but studies showed that this is not optimal for everyone. For instance, children need anywhere between 12,000 to 15,000 steps a day and people in recovery from illness, less. In fact, adults have obvious benefits from a thirty- minute brisk walk a few times a week.

10.000 steps a day is not equal to physical exercise!

Resistance training is one way to stay in a peak mental and physical state. Specialists advise between 2 to 3 times a week and 3 to 4 sets per body part with 8 to 12 reps.

In older age, lighter weight and higher reps with a two-day rest between training has shown the best results.

I enjoy weight resistance training, which keeps my mind and body at optimal levels. For middle-aged men, over 50 years old, professionals recommend gym training sessions, in-order to avoid the onset of sarcopenia - the degenerative loss of skeletal muscle mass and strength that begins in middle age.

Loss of muscle mass is detrimental for both sexes as it can lead to ailments and disorders. The naturally produced hormone testosterone is the main reason men would do well to lift weights, as testosterone is found in muscles.

Craig and his colleagues (1989), measured levels of growth hormone and testosterone in twenty - three - year olds and sixty-three year olds, before and after a resistance strength training program. An increase of both hormones was found in all the participants at the end of the program. (Engage in weight resistance strength training only after seeking medical advice).

Muscle loss is due to a decrease in the male hormone testosterone, which contributes to sex drive, thinking ability, mood and quality of life. Vitamins, minerals and supplements might help some individuals when participating in any exercise regime. Studies on the effects of consuming a daily multivitamin are not conclusive.

Men and women might benefit from consuming 1g to 1.2g of protein per body kg, in their daily diet when active in physical exercise. I believe supplements are only an addition to the foundation of a healthy meal plan.

Positive self-image
A guide on health for Canada (2009) found some interesting facts regarding self-positive body image.

Weight centered

Dieting
Restrictive eating
Counting calories
Yo-yo diets
Eating disorders

Exercise
No pain, no gain
Burn calories
Hard-core, 3 times weekly

Self–dissatisfaction
Unrealistic goals
Weight obsession
Fat phobia
Perfection (10)

Vitality

Healthy Eating
Pleasure in variety of foods
Lower fat and complex carbs
Energy nutrient foods
Listen to hunger cues

Active lifestyle
Moderate and fun activities
Activity – your way
Do it for joy of feeling
Enjoy an active lifestyle

Positive-self & body image
Acceptance of differences
Appreciate strengths
Tolerance of other shapes
Enjoy your uniqueness

Feel good about yourself
It seems as if the entire world is focusing on body shape and size. This can lead to various mental disorders like anorexia, bulimia and unhealthy low levels of self-esteem. By learning to accept ourselves and building a confident and realistic body image we open a path to higher self-esteem.

Experiencing mixed feelings about our body image is normal for many. Practices of self-compassion, education on the topic and self-understanding helps towards making healthier choices in eating and exercise habits.

Without meaning to compare your body to a mere machine, I would like you to imagine that you have just bought your dream supercar:

What fuel would you use?

Budget, or the best you can afford?

The media are constantly emphasizing the highly concerning increases in obesity. The eight glasses of water a day and five fruit and vegetable guidelines along with the latest fad diets have confused us. Without mentioning the detailed amounts of carbs, fats and proteins needed daily for optimal health and well-being (individual amounts differ), it is clear why the *Mediterranean diet* is one of the better options.

Research has shown that the olive oil, fresh fruit, legumes, cereals and seafood full of omega-3s found in the Mediterranean diet is the main reason for lower mortality rates. Other benefits include fewer cases of Parkinson's and disease, with an overall positive effect on mood and well-being.

The Chinese say:

"We often dig our own graves with our teeth."

Who would you blame for neglecting your own body?

Warren Buffett addressing a group of high school students:

"When I was sixteen, I had just two things on my mind - girls and cars. I wasn't very good with girls. So, I thought about cars. I thought about girls, too, but I had more luck with cars.

Let's say that when I turned sixteen, a genie had appeared to me. And that genie said, 'Warren, I'm going to give you the car of your choice. It'll be here tomorrow morning with a big bow tied on it. Brand-new. And it's all yours.'
Having heard all the genie stories, I would say, 'What's the catch?' And the genie would answer, 'There's only one catch. This is the last car you're ever going to get in your life. So, it's got to last a lifetime.

If that had happened, I would have picked out that car. But, can you imagine, knowing it had to last a lifetime, what I would do with it?

I would read the manual about five times. I would always keep it garaged. If there was the least little dent or scratch, I'd have it fixed right away because I wouldn't want it rusting. I would baby that car, because it would have to last a lifetime. That's exactly the position you are in concerning your mind and body.

You only get one mind and one body!

And it's got to last a lifetime. Now, it's very easy to let them ride for many years. But if you don't take care of that mind

*and that body, they'll be a wreck forty years later, just like the
car would be.*

*It's what you do right now, today, that determines how your
mind and body will operate ten, twenty, and thirty years
from now."*

Additional notes

Since being introduced to an active lifestyle at twelve, I
have taken part in many types of exercise. Listening to my
body has helped me live an injury free and joyful life.
Positivity is something I live and breathe and it's only
possible for me by sleeping well, exercising two to three
times a week and eating *sensibly*. That means no strict diets
or calorie reducing programs, just thoughtful eating. These
are all prerequisites for boosting serotonin levels.

Positivity isn't achievable without a healthy body, just as
it's not possible with an unhealthy mind and healthy body.
Due to my frequent contact with fitness professionals, I
often come across great bodies with troubled minds and
when I say troubled, I mean frustrated. Motivational fitness
training videos for some individuals are great and for
others they may prove harmful.

The teenagers of today are highly vulnerable to the
dangers linked with perfect images *(often filtered)* in social
networks. This stems from the innate human desire of
wanting to be liked.

Obsessively checking the number of likes on social network platforms might lead to self-harming behavior in striving towards the perfect "picture".

Building healthy self-esteem through exercise is one path provided you don't endanger your health. If governments want fewer obese and sick people, how about endorsing health supplements and providing gym or sports center discounts?

THE BELLY AND THE MEMBERS

The members of the Body once rebelled against the Belly, who, they said, led an idle, lazy life at their expense. The Hands declared that they would not again lift a crust even to keep him from starving, the Mouth that it would not take in a bit more food, the Legs that they would carry him about no longer, and so on with the others.

The Belly quietly allowed them to follow their own courses, well knowing that they would all soon come to their senses, as indeed they did, when, for want of the blood and nourishment supplied from the stomach, they found themselves fast becoming mere skin and bone.

Balance is the key to everything.

"To keep the body in good health is a duty... otherwise we shall not be able to keep our mind strong and clear."
-Buddha.

CHAPTER 6

PERSONALITY (WHO AM I?)

"Know thyself"
-*Socrates* (470–399 BC)

Is a well-known aphorism in personality development. Because everyone is different! Psychologists describe personality as:

A set of characteristics, patterns of thoughts, feelings and behaviors that make a person unique.

Multiple personality tests are available to individuals and organizations where the most common assessment methods are:

Self-report inventories
Test-takers read questions and rate how well the question applies to them. They have their own unique strengths and weaknesses. One of their benefits is the ease of standardization, reliability and validity, which is better than:

Projective tests
Give a scene to interpret.
Weaknesses – mood or wanting to impress others could influence results.

People take personality tests for a variety of reasons including: Choosing an identity, justifying behavior, positive feedback on view of self, assess personality theories, diagnose psychological problems, screen job candidates and look at personality changes.

Deciding on a test is a matter of preference. I will address three of the most popular personality assessments.

But first, how did we get so many personality tests, which assess everything from neuroticism to agreeableness?

There are four major theories that contributed to contemporary personality assessments, which include famous psychologists like Sigmund Freud and Carl Rogers.

Four major theories
Psychoanalytic – unconscious, childhood, id, ego, superego. *Sigmund Freud, Erik Erikson, Carl Jung, Alfred Adler, Karen Horney.*

Humanistic – free will, experience, hierarchy of needs. *Carl Rogers, Abraham Maslow.*

Trait – number of broad theories, extrovert/introvert/ neurotic. *Hans Eysenck, Raymond Cattell, Robert McCrae and Paul Costa.*

Social Cognitive - influence of environment, conditioning, observation, competencies. *Albert Bandura, Walter Mischel.*

A combination of the four major theories contributed to multiple personality tests. I took three of the most well-known personality tests: MBTI, DISC and BIG FIVE.

Myers and Briggs Type Indicator (MBTI)
Measures Aspects of Personality.

MBTI originated from Carl Jung's 1921 book on types of personalities and behavior prediction. Katharine Cook Briggs and her daughter Isabel Briggs Myers developed a method based on Jung's theories to decipher a wide range of behaviors.

The purpose of the test is to identify people's preferences, improve their behavior and communication skills with other types. In addition, knowing your type could also help you choose a career that matches your personality.

The modern MBTI psychological test splits personalities into four dimensions and classifies people into sixteen patterns (types).

They are all interpreted with a four-letter acronym e.g. ESFP:

Energizing: Where you get your energy:

a) Extrovert = *Energy from outside world, activities, people.*

b) Introvert = *Energy from the inner world, emotions, ideas.*

Participation: How you take in information:

a) Sensing = *Use sense to determine what is real.*

b) Intuition = *Use imagination to sense what is real.*

Decision: How you make decisions:

a) Thinking = *Organize information for logical decisions.*

b) Feeling = *Organize information for personal decisions.*

Living: Your desired way of life:

a) Judging = *Like an organized and planned life.*

b) Perceiving = *Prefer a spontaneous and flexible life.*

Example: You're going out Friday night…

E's = will tell everyone.

N's = will try a new restaurant.

T's = decide on venue-based value, reviews.

J's = will book a week in advance.

I's = unlikely to mention it.

S's = go to their usual.

F's = will do whatever everyone else wants.

P's = will decide when they leave the house.

Even-though the MBTI mentions weaknesses, this popular assessment highlights our good features. Keep in mind we tend to find what we are looking for, just like in a zodiac sign horoscope.

Carl Jung believed individuals prefer one of two functions for processing data and coming to conclusions:

Thinking or Feeling.
- *Thinkers* prefer logic and objectivity.
- *Feelers* prefer personal values and subjectivity.

Thinkers and feelers arrive at different conclusions because of the criteria they use to evaluate information.

Is the research scientific? Yes.

Is it fun? Yes.

Will I find parts of me in the test? Yes.

Should I limit my personality to four letters? No.

We are all much more than any self-report test. However, the MBTI is a good general explanatory guide of why we behave the way we do in certain situations.

TIP!

If you are looking for a fun, free and anonymous MBTI assessment, visit my site at: *www.thepositiveacademy.net*

DISC

Focuses Primarily on Behavior.

Do you consider yourself - dominant or passive?

Are you more outgoing or reserved?

Are you calm and steady or easily overexcited?

DISC aims to answer types of behavior and is a well-known personality/behavioral assessment. However, it is restricted to the working environment.

The initial Disc model originated from Dr William Marston's book *"Emotions of Normal People"* (1928). But, just like Carl Jung, Marston did not create a measuring instrument to test his theories.

The plethora of DISC tests and their easy interpretation has made the assessment a popular choice in organizations.

The DISC test divides behavior into four main sections, which everyone has some of, but in different amounts.

However, a few tendencies explain your approach to life and daily behavior:

- Outgoing
- Reserved
- Task-oriented
- People-oriented

(D) Dominant – Dominance - *Outgoing* = Task oriented, accomplishing tasks, making things happen, gets to the bottom line quick.

(I) Inspiring – Influence - *Outgoing* = People oriented, loves interaction, socializing, having fun, focused on what others think of them.

(S) Supportive – Steadiness - *Reserved* = People oriented, enjoys relationships, helps, supports others, works well in a team.

(C) Cautious – Conscientiousness - *Reserved* = Task oriented, seeks value, consistent, focuses on accuracy, looks for accuracy.

The various DISC assessments give you a percentage in each of the four categories, along with tips on how to best deal with other temperament types.

Typical behaviors from a person high in:

Dominance:
Broad viewer
Arrogant
Competitive

Influence:
Enthusiastic
Optimistic
Collaborator

Steadiness:
Calm
Supportive
Humble

Conscientiousness:
Objective
Independent
Tactful

DISC is a personality test, which reveals how we handle professional life issues, tasks and daily activities.

BIG FIVE (OCEAN)
Stable characteristics

The Big Five assessment differs from the MBTI and DISC tests, as it's based on trait theory (stable characteristics). Many personality researchers agree on the OCEAN, or big five core personality dimensions.

Decades of personality research building on Cattell's (1940s) 16 factors and based on Goldberg's (1981) model, led to McCrae and Costa's (1987) validation of the most mainstream and accepted framework of personality in psychology.

Each of the five personality factors represents a range between two extremes i.e. *extroversion – introversion.*

Range is the key word in the big five assessment in that most people lie somewhere between each dimension. The five categories in the big five or OCEAN are:

Openness – Imaginative, multiple interests, insightful.
    High openness = Creative, abstract thinking.
    Low openness = Dislikes change, resists new ideas.

Conscientiousness – Self-disciplined, consistent.
    High conscientiousness = Attention to detail.
    Low conscientiousness = Messy, careless.

Extraversion – Sociable, assertive, talkative, expressive.
    High extraversion = Easily makes new friends.
    Low extraversion = Quiet, introspective.

Agreeableness – Trusting, altruistic, kind, affectionate.
    High agreeableness = Empathetic, caring.
    Low agreeableness = Sarcastic, antagonistic.

Neuroticism – *Moody, sad, unstable, awkward.*
High neuroticism = Anxious, jealous.
Low neuroticism = Relaxed, confident.

The range of OCEAN'S universal classification includes both *nature* and *nurture*. Multiple research has shown that the big five traits are stable during adulthood. Older age has shown a correlation with a decrease in extraversion, and openness to experience.

The findings make sense, as when people mature they become more selective and set/comfortable in their ways. However, the two things that increase as people get older, are agreeableness and conscientiousness.

Getting to know ourselves through different personality inventories is a fun pastime and just that. The essence of any assessment is to encourage you not to be hard on yourself and to avoid negative self-talk.

We can only achieve by first believing and then acting. Personality is complex, and that's it's attractive force, because it makes us all unique.

TIP!
If you are looking for a free and anonymous BIG FIVE assessment, visit my site: *www.thepositiveacademy.net*
All three tests (MBTI, DISC, BIG FIVE) describe generic strengths and weaknesses of specific types or traits. Multiple

other personality assessments can show an inclination towards an occupation, which can be a fun read.

The assessments' recommended jobs are as good as they can be, in a self-report questionnaire. I am sure you've all met people who like crunching numbers, while others need frequent social contact. Most jobs these days require transferrable skills in communication, research, planning, human relations, organization, management, leadership, etc.

The choice is yours to make the most of your current level of skills and ability.

Additional notes

Personality assessments are commonplace in most companies for vetting the right candidates. Businesses use specific personality tests according to previous experience or HR recommendations.

Organizations will hire to fulfil their immediate needs.

Personality assessments will reveal your intuitive thoughts and extra characteristics. I like to take them to discover the latest innovative personality questionnaire methods.

Personality is complex, and this is the reason employers use boxes to place people in categories. Every one of us is so much more than any personality test with an abundance to give to the world. Most of us know if we gain energy from others (extrovert), or energy from being alone (introvert).

I like lecturing, facilitating, or addressing a big audience, but I also enjoy a bit of quite time in solitude. Opportunities to show your social fun side, or thoughtful, introspective self are vast. People's needs and desires change with age and so do their goals and pleasure-seeking activities.

Provided you retain a healthy body and mind, the child in every one of you keeps dreaming. Life is all about expecting a better tomorrow, but most important of all enjoying your current path.

"We are all born with a unique genetic blueprint, which lays out the basic characteristics of our personality, as well as our physical health and appearance... And yet, we all know that life experiences do change us." –Joan D. Vinge.

C H A P T E R 7

STRENGTHS AND VIRTUES

"Everybody is a genius. But if you judge a fish by its ability to climb a tree, it will live its whole life believing that its stupid."
-Albert Einstein (1879-1955).

Do you know your strengths? I've asked this question countless times of people from all walks of life. The answer is usually:

"I don't know" or *"Cooking, cycling, tennis, hiking…"*

However, when I specifically ask about personality strengths, the answers vary from hardworking, loyal, reliable, perfectionist, or even lazy, maybe a personal strength for some.

A)   So, how can we discover our personal (character) strengths and not a learned activity, skill, or assumption of character?

B)   What is the point of knowing what you are good at?

C)   How can it help you with your life in a professional and personal context?

By discovering your personality strengths and virtues (values in life), the social activities you take part in, and choice of occupation, will become more enjoyable and fulfilling.

Why?

Because you are working to your strengths.

Here are ten good reasons for discovering and building your strengths:

1.   Using your strengths **makes you happier.** Studies have found that people who use their strengths have higher levels of well-being (subjective and psychological). Using your strengths in new and different ways every day is linked to higher levels of happiness and lower levels of depression.

2.   Using your strengths **makes you more confident.** Research has found that people who use their strengths more report higher levels of self-efficacy (confidence), believing that they can achieve their goals.

3.   Using your strengths **results in higher self-esteem.** Developing strengths can help people improve

their self-esteem in just a matter of weeks. Studies have found that the use of strengths has been linked to higher levels of self-esteem.

4. Using your strengths **gives you more energy and vitality.** Utilising your strengths is associated with higher levels of psychological vitality (energy).

5. Using your strengths **decreases stress levels.** Research has found that the use of strengths has been shown to be associated with lower levels of stress. Higher strengths = lower stress.

6. Using your strengths **makes you more resilient.** The use of strengths correlates with resilience and adventure. Using your strengths and going outside your comfort zone can build your resilience.

7. Using your strengths **makes you more likely to achieve** your goals. It has been found that people who use their strengths are more likely to achieve their goals with more satisfaction.

8. Using your strengths **helps you perform better at work.** A study has found that managers who emphasize performance and personal strengths resulted in higher performance rates, whereas emphasizing weaknesses decreased performance rates.

9. Using your strengths **helps you to be more engaged** in work. Work engagement has been found to increase when people focus on developing their strengths. Focusing on strengths is a core predictor in workplace engagement.

10. Using your strengths **helps you personally develop and grow.** Studies have found that focusing on strengths (rather than weaknesses) helps people with their self-development. Leaders that focus on their personal and team's development through strengths see higher benefits and increased success.

Positive psychology views character strengths and talents as two separate entities that when aligned can make your life more joyful.

Character strengths – The *"how"* we like to work, which is visible in behaviors and is aligned with our values.
Talents – The *"what"* we like to do in our work and be recognized for in our jobs.

In this chapter I will describe the psychological strengths (ingredients) that a person possesses reliant on their virtues.

Empirical studies from renowned personality development researchers Seligman, Peterson, Buckingham, the Gallup organization, multiple inventories, personal ads, lyrics and historical figures like Benjamin Franklin, William Bennet and Sir John Templeton and all the major religion and philosophical traditions resulted in the classification of six universal core moral virtues, divided into twenty-four signature character strengths:

Wisdom and Knowledge
Cognitive strengths through acquiring and using knowledge.

Creativity: Originality, artistic achievement, adaptivity.

Curiosity: Interest in a new experience, exploring, openness.

Judgement: Critical thinking, thinking things, open-minded.

Love of Learning: Mastering new skills, adding knowledge.

Perspective: Providing wise counsel, big picture view.

Courage
Emotional strengths that exercise will to accomplish goals in face of competition.

Bravery: Not shrinking from fear, speaking up for rights.

Perseverance: Persistence, industrious, finishing what you start.

Honesty: Authenticity, speaking the truth, integrity, sincerity.

Zest: Enthusiasm, energy, approaching life with excitement.

Humanity
Interpersonal strengths including taking care of and debriefing others.

Love: Loving and being loved, caring, being close to people.

Kindness: Generous, altruistic, niceness, compassion, helpful.

Social Intelligence: Awareness of motives/feelings of others.

Justice
Civic strengths that underlie a healthy community life.

Teamwork: Working in groups, loyal, social, citizenship.

Fairness: Treating people the same, non-biased decisions, just.

Leadership: Organizing groups, activities, encouragement.

Temperance
Strengths that protect against excess.

Forgiveness: Mercy, giving second chances, forgiving people.

Humility: Modesty, letting accomplishments speak for you.

Prudence: Careful, not taking undue risks, cautious.

Self-regulation: Self-control, disciplined, regulating emotions.

Transcendence
Strengths that forge connections to the larger universe and provide meaning.

Appreciation of beauty and excellence: Awe, nature, art, math.

Gratitude: Thankful for good things, expressing thanks.

Hope: Optimism, best future, future-mindedness, a bright future.

Humor: Playfulness, liking to laugh, tease, bringing smiles.

Spirituality: Religiousness, a faith, a higher purpose, meaning.

Interestingly, gender studies on character strengths showed: **Women** scoring highest on honesty, kindness, love, gratitude and fairness. **Men** scoring highest on hope, humor, gratitude, curiosity and honesty.

Can we conclude from current research that men and women inherit characteristics?

or

Is it upbringing that shapes them? That is still up for debate…

The one thing that's certain is the increase of life satisfaction levels in both genders when they live a life according to their strengths.

TIP!
Before taking the highly recommended 240 question self-report free character strengths and virtues online test (Peterson and Seligman, 2004) at *www.authentichappiness. org*, see which of these comments live within you.

- **Childhood memories**: What do you remember doing as a child that you still do now – but most likely much better? Strengths often have deep roots in our early lives.

- **Energy**: What activities give you an energetic buzz when you are doing them? These activities are very likely calling on your strengths.

- **Authenticity**: When do you feel most like the "real you"? The chances are that you'll be using your strengths.

- **Ease**: See what activities come naturally to you, the ones you excel in, apparently without a lot of effort. These will probably be your strengths.

- **Rapid learning**: What are the things you have picked up quickly, learning them almost effortlessly? Rapid learning often shows an underlying strength.

- **"To do" lists**: Notice the things that never make it on your "to do" list. These things that always seem to get done often reveal an underlying strength that means we never need to be asked twice.

I look at life this way:

There are things you can do something about, so do them!
The things out of your control, let them be!

The character strengths and virtues assessment resonate in many personal and professional dimensions.

We spend half of our adult waking life in a job, so why not work to our strengths?

Additional notes

As far back as I can remember I've used my signature character strengths without consciously knowing about them.

It's probably the reason I believe life is neither easy nor hard, but just what you make it. We all must deal with undesirable events. The "*getting back on the saddle as soon as you fall*" metaphor is best put in practice when working to your strengths.

The trick could well be to discover your character strengths as early as possible and to enhance them. It's only natural to enjoy doing things you are good at, as some side effects include: success, appreciation, good relationships and a more fulfilling life.

Who likes to be put down continuously for not being good enough, smart enough, tough enough etc.? Life is not a Hollywood movie, but a dynamic and fluid theatre play, where you are the main character and director.

So, write, direct and act your life story well, with plenty of zest, vigor, enthusiasm and joy.

VALUE

A popular speaker started off a seminar by holding up a $20 bill.

A crowd of 200 had gathered to hear him speak. He asked,

"Who would like this $20 bill?"

Two hundred hands went up.
He said, "I will give this $20 to one of you but first, let me do this." He crumpled the bill up.

He then asked, "Who still wants it?"

All two hundred hands were still raised.

"Well," he replied, "What if I do this?" Then he dropped the bill on the ground and stomped on it with his shoes.

He picked it up and showed it to the crowd. The bill was all crumpled and dirty.

"Now who still wants it?"

All the hands still went up.

My friends, I have just showed you a very important lesson. No matter what I did to the money, you still wanted it because it did not decrease in value. It was still worth $20. Many times, in our lives, life crumples us and grinds us into the dirt. We make bad decisions or deal with poor circumstances. We feel worthless. But no matter what has happened or what will happen, you will never lose your value. You are special – Never forget it!

CHAPTER 8

POSITIVE SELF-IMAGE / PSYCHO-CYBERNETICS

"Our self-image, strongly held, determines what we become."
- Maxwell Maltz (1889-1975).

Dr Maltz brought awareness to self-image and our well-being with Psycho-Cybernetics.

"To accomplish great things, we must not only act but also dream, not only plan but also believe."
-Anatole France *(1844-1924),* French novelist.

Your self-image is how you see and feel about yourself. However, this can change regardless of your age. It all begins with developing awareness around your thoughts. Start by concentrating on your previous successes and bring them into the present moment to gain self-esteem. At first this requires conscious effort, but in time it becomes a mental habit.

You have a success mechanism within you that will steer your mind to a productive goal if you allow it.

Think back to when you were a child learning a new task. Did you recall how many times you tried before succeeding?

How many times did you fall off your bike?

You are the product of your imagination and you can use it either constructively, or destructively. If you think well of yourself and have that confidence in yourself, you will succeed. If you think in negative terms, you will fail – unless you change your self-image.

"Everything depends upon your concept of yourself."
-Maxwell Maltz.

Often this is the impact of past personal experiences, teachers, parents or other figures in your life. This continues to chip away at your confidence and triggers self-doubt. However, this can change. Start the process by focusing only on your successes.

A mistake doesn't make a failure, for success is learning how to rise above failure.

It is your own opinion that counts most!

Dr. Maxwell Maltz wrote a wonderful book called *Psycho-Cybernetics* in the 1960s, where he coined the phrase: 21 days to form a new habit. He came up with the number twenty-one because that was the time it took on average his patients to recover from plastic surgery procedures.

Since then, the twenty-one-day habit forming method is practiced by many life coaches.

Here are the twelve core lessons in Psycho –Cybernetics for defining and achieving your goals and building a positive self-image:

1) Your Self-image
Your self-image, how you see and feel about yourself, can be changed at any time regardless of your age. This begins with developing awareness around your thoughts. It's a process of retraining (and expanding) your mind. As you do this, refuse to focus on (or mention) any negative statement about yourself. It's the negative statements that continue to belittle your self-image. While doing this, turn your back on the failures of the past. Then concentrate on your previous successes as you bring them into the present moment. At first this requires a conscious effort but in time becomes a mental habit. This aids with replacing the negative thoughts with a newer and greater self-image.

2) Success Mechanism
You have a success mechanism within you that will steer

your mind to a productive goal if you allow it. Think back
to when you were a child learning a new task. Did you
recall how many times you tried before succeeding? You
continued to repeat and practice until you could do the
thing you sought out to do.

As an adult, it's no different. It's like having a small recorder
in your brain that continues to repeat what you play, so
you must become conscious of what you are playing. This
requires daily observation. Once you are aware of what
you are playing about yourself you can make the effort to
change it. Your subconscious mind does what it is directed
to do, and always knows; it only needs to be directed in a
way that brings you success and happiness.

3) Your Imagination
You are the product of your imagination and you can
use it either constructively, or destructively. If you think
well of yourself and have that confidence in yourself, you
will succeed. If you think in negative terms you will fail
– *unless you change your self-image.* You start the process
by focusing only on your successes while shifting your
perception around the fears of failure. An important
note here is that it is the opinion of yourself that counts,
nothing else. Knowing this, you can learn how to use your
imagination constructively to change your self-image, by
visualizing yourself as you desire to be on a continual basis.

4) Creative Thought and Action

Change your mind to think and act creatively. You can learn to reach your goal by exercising your success mechanism daily and refusing to be side-tracked by negative feelings. You enhance this by focusing only on your accomplishments of the past while remaining in the present. In doing this you are no longer side-tracked by negative feelings or past stories. Keep your environment pure. If the situation in the present defies a solution, then sleep ON it – not WITH it. In doing that you commit your success mechanism to work subconsciously while you sleep. You initiate this by focusing on the problem prior to sleep knowing the solution will be provided. Repeat this until it becomes clear and you will create programs that automatically work for you while you sleep, allowing you to wake with the solutions.

5) The Art of Relaxation

Learn how to relax your mind and your body by connecting to yourself. When the mind is in a relaxed state its more receptive. This makes it easier to program success in your subconscious mind just like you would program a computer. To begin the process of relaxation you start with forgiveness, that is, forgiveness of yourself *and* others. Then see yourself as a person of great confidence, independent of circumstances or things. Cease to compare yourself to others. Only compare you to you, that is your present self to your past self, and you will see your growth and progress which feeds your confidence. It is equally important to release all chronic frustration. Everyone has frustration during the day, but chronic frustration is due to the problems of yesterday that you continue and carry with you like a pack of weights on your back. These repetitive past feelings need to be released and this is done by living fully in the present. Begin your days with a few minutes of silence as you sit with yourself and observe. This will help you release the painful emotions of the past for healing and aid with relaxing the mind and body in order to dissolve anxiety.

6) The Power of Beliefs

Your beliefs can either be true or false, but if you believe them you will act that part. *Beliefs become habits and habits are nothing more than self-hypnosis.* So, it's important to learn how to de-hypnotize yourself from those negative beliefs. Begin this process by focusing ONLY on your success while remaining in the present moment. This is a mental exercise that consists of bringing your success from all past experiences into the present moment. Then create a clear picture of how you wish to see yourself and focus on that daily. As you continue you will find your opinion of yourself changes as your self-image expands and your confidence increases.

7) Quest for Happiness

Happiness is a habit, and it's just as easy to be happy as it is to be unhappy. It is simply a cycle of thoughts that increases through love and self-acceptance. This begins with the understanding that happiness belongs to you. Happiness is an inward state of being that is independent of circumstances, people, or things. Make it a conscious effort to focus on your successes while incorporating self-compliments. Expand on your happiness with love for yourself and others. Repeat these mental exercises daily until they become mental habits. As your self-image increases you will find a greater love within yourself which feeds your inner state of joy.

8) Success Mechanism Phases

Here are the phases of the success mechanism that allow your self-image to grow as tall as you want to be. Branch out from the word success and return to each of these aspects as often as possible:

- Sense of Direction, your goals
- Understanding of your needs and others
- Courage
- Compassion
- Esteem, self-respect
- Self-acceptance, you are somebody regardless of your mistakes
- Self-Confidence.

9) Self-image Failure Mechanism

Here are the aspects of the failure mechanism which scar your self-image. Through this awareness you can learn how to avoid future scarring of your self-image by making a conscious effort to release these.

- Frustration
- Aggressiveness
- Insecurity
- Loneliness
- Uncertainty
- Resentment
- Emptiness

10) Releasing Emotional Scaring

Remember that you are too big to be threatened. By facing your fears safely in your imagination, you will free yourself from them. Learn how to become self-reliant as this will help you to coach yourself through the process. Take the time to focus on your mind and body as you relax into your being. Learn to let go of the past, releasing all emotional scaring so you no longer carry the old baggage with you into the present. Make a conscious effort to apply these techniques daily in a relaxed state of mind and you will see your self-image grow and expand.

11) Managing Stress

Learn how to stand up to stress through effective use of your imagination. You do this by changing every crisis into an opportunity, by shifting how you think about each crisis as you change your approach and action. What you focus on expands. By shifting your focus, you can learn to transform the stress into motivation. Your mind will guide you if you allow it and this is greatly enhanced through meditation and visualization.

12) Attention and Focus

You can change your luck by refusing to allow your negative feelings to impact your self-image. You do this by concentrating on the confidence of the past as you bring that into the present moment whenever a negative feeling arises. You embrace and release the negative feelings, while changing your point of focus. In doing this, the old mental habits transform into positive mental habits that work *for* you. You become a success when you **learn to be yourself**. Select realistic goals to reach fulfilment and exercise your creative success mechanism daily to achieve them. Combine thought with creative performance and action as you train yourself to remain present with everything you do.

Everything starts within and anything is changeable. Along with the natural process of aging, our body shape changes whether we like it or not. Our sleeping patterns, eating habits and frequency of exercise are great tools for sculpting a strong mind, body and spirit. Social media is full of body transformations (visual changes) which also affect the thinking patterns of the person too.

So, how can our brains and thinking patterns change? We are our habits, but many PET and MRI scans have shown that our brain wiring could do with a positive tune-up every now and then. Change can benefit us or prohibit us from being in our best physical and mental state. Let's look at some scientific evidence on change, or plasticity in the human brain.

I am referring to the famous study of London's black cab drivers (2011).

London black cab drivers

The industrious 21,000 London cabbies are part of the transport lifeline of the English capital. Every black cab, driver in central London must gain "The Knowledge"–a memorized map of the 8.5 million inhabitants in the capital. The knowledge certificate includes some 25,000 streets and thousands of landmarks right down to the order of theatres in Shaftesbury Avenue.

The learning process takes three to four years to complete, with a final test - "The London Examination System" - that can often take twelve attempts to pass. Even then, only about 50% of trainee cabbies ace the exam.

A report in the journal *Current Biology (2011)*, published the structural changes in the brain caused during the process of learning the mental atlas of London. Results showed effects on memory along with a creation of a greater volume of nerve cells in the brain's hippocampus.

This was the concluding statement of the researchers after

the study of thirty-nine trainee cabbies:

"The human brain remains plastic even in adult life, allowing it to adapt when we learn new tasks."

That said, there will always be people with a higher predisposition to succeed in certain tasks, which includes memorizing central London faster.

Change can only occur when knowledge turns into action.

Our mind-map could be one of positive or negative wiring. The template of learning a new language is like learning new thinking, interpreting or different behavioral patterns. The London black cab taxi driver study is one example from a rich bundle of information on possible and long-lasting positive change. We all have an internal power to find what we are looking for, provided something motivates us to do so.

Some people have more grit than others, and that's fine. Others need certain conditions or environments, and some would greatly benefit from a life coach. How you do it is individual. Finding your way to higher self-esteem is a mental, physical and spiritual process.

Additional notes
A life without self-esteem is like living in the shadows. It surprises me when I ask teenagers about role models and

they say they don't have any.

I gained inspiration from Hollywood movie actors, sportsmen and pop singers when a teenager. My driving force was to develop my mind and body the best I could through vivid imagination, passion, exercise and perseverance.

Inspiration can be derived from scientists, inventors, architects, mathematicians, historians, archaeologists, sports icons, teachers, family members, etc. The list is endless.

Enhancing your self-esteem is key to the quality of life you lead, regardless of how many riches you might acquire. Low self-esteem brings on feelings of jealousy, anger, inadequacy, self-harm and depression to name just a few. These are all non-money-related ailments.

In our modern era of video-gamers and social network addicts, higher self-esteem is important for everyone. Personal circumstance changes, such as giving birth, divorce, job loss, getting older, or sickness can affect our levels of self-esteem.

It is our responsibility as human beings to enhance our own self-esteem, and the self-esteem of the people dear to us.
A life with high self-esteem is friendly and joyful.

BIRD ON A BRANCH

A tired bird landed on a branch. The bird rested, enjoying the view from the branch and the protection it offered from dangerous animals. Just as the bird became used to the branch and the support and safety it offered, a strong wind started blowing, and the tree swayed with such intensity that it seemed the branch would snap in half.

*But the bird was not worried for it knew two important truths. **The first truth** – even without the branch it was able to fly, and thus remain safe through the power of its own two wings. **The second truth** – it also knew that there were many other branches upon which it could temporarily rest.*

A bird sitting on a tree isn't afraid of the branch breaking because its trust is not on the branch but in its wings, so believe in yourself and win the world.

"To establish true self-esteem, we must concentrate on our successes and forget about the failures and the negatives in our lives." –Denis Waitle.

CHAPTER 9

GRATITUDE, SAVORING AND MINDFULNESS

Positive psychology identifies gratitude, mindfulness and savoring as three essential practices for positive living.

People associate gratitude with saying 'Thank you.' Psychologists view gratitude as an emotion.

We can feel and express gratitude in multiple ways.

Applying gratitude:
Past - retrieving positive memories and being thankful for elements of childhood or past blessings.
Present - not taking good fortune for granted as it comes.
Future - maintaining a hopeful and optimistic attitude.

Regardless of your inherent or current level of gratitude, it's a quality that can be cultivated. The belief in many psychology circles is that being grateful is a deep appreciation for someone or something, which produces longer lasting positivity.

There are also differences between mindfulness and savoring:

Mindfulness is the practice of focusing attention on the present moment and accepting it without judgement.

Savoring is the awareness of pleasure as it occurs and deliberate conscious attention to the experience of pleasure. First, let's start with a detailed definition of **gratitude** and the two stages involved in feelings of gratitude.

Gratitude
The acknowledgement of goodness in one's life:
- The affirmation that all is good in life.
- Saying yes to life.
- Acknowledging something that gratifies us both in its presence and by the effort to choose it.

Recognising that sources of goodness are outside the self:

Being grateful to other people, animals, the world, not to self.

Recognising who to thank for the goodness in our-lives.

What is the purpose of gratitude?

Expressing gratitude enhances an overall sense of well-being. The more grateful you are the more likely that you are agreeable and less neurotic. Gratitude also acts as a bond to strengthen relationship connections and life satisfaction. Emmons and McCullough (2003) found a 25% increase in levels of optimism after a ten-week period of study on gratitude focus in daily life.

From better physical and mental health, stronger self-control, to an overall better life, gratitude practices have shown to increase many health-related ingredients to living positive.

What is a good way to apply gratitude?

You can practise gratitude every evening before going to sleep by thinking of the positive things that happened during the day.

Here are other practices that have shown to increase gratitude:

Journaling: Once a week writing in a journal a few positive things that happened to you, or you are grateful for.

Gratitude Walk: Observing the things around you see on a walk, while cleansing your mind of other thoughts. Take in the smells and sounds of nature, trees, plants, chirping of birds, etc.

Gratitude letter: Write a hand-written letter to a person you are grateful for having in your life. Detailed points of why you are grateful to them and how they affected your life has shown a raise in gratitude levels, especially when the letter is delivered personally.

Keeping a gratitude journal: Making notes is good practice to reflect on things later. Some studies have shown journals to be more effective at the end of the week instead of every evening. The great thing about gratitude is that it can be practised anywhere, anytime.

I express gratitude multiple times throughout the day; when I'm driving, consulting, eating, or pausing for a small break while I write this chapter. Being grateful for who you are, where you are, what you have, or what others have done for you etc. takes only a few seconds. The positive emotion dividends are priceless.

Many times, I feel appreciative of little things like a walk in a park, reading a book or tasting ice-cream. Closing your front door, preparing warm food, running a bath, or choosing the way you want to live life, are all things that many of us can reflect on and be grateful for.

Are you grateful for what you have?

Are you grateful for who you are?

or

Do you take things for granted?

Do you feel dissatisfied?

Take a moment out of what you are doing right now…
Feel blessed for where you are…

What you have…

Where your future is going…

You don't need to live in a big house, drive an expensive car, or have the body of a Greek god/goddess to feel grateful. Simple things like looking out of a window or enjoying a warm cup of tea can evoke feelings of comfort and gratefulness.

Taking time out from staring at the screen, or paperwork and looking away up at the sky, taking a stroll in a forest, watching children play, listening to pleasant music, or breathing in deeply, costs nothing.

The options of practiced gratitude are countless where precious seconds of good feelings (gratefulness) can provide you with the energy to *seize the day.*

Savoring

Savoring is the awareness of pleasure and of consciously paying attention to the experience of pleasure. Savoring involves cognitive and behavioral processes that regulate positive feelings. Meaning, thoughts and behaviors influence the frequency, intensity and duration of a positive experience.

Two experts on the effects of savoring, Fred Bryant and Joseph Veroff (2007), discovered three preferred time frames of savoring:

Past – reminiscing about pleasures we enjoyed in the past.
Present – savoring life's pleasures in the present.
Future – anticipating future pleasant events.

Here are five techniques to enhance savoring:

Sharing with others: seek people to share the experience and tell others how much you value the moment. This is the single strongest predictor of the level of pleasure.

Memory building: take mental photographs, or even a physical souvenir of the event, and reminisce about it later with others.

Self-congratulation: don't be afraid of pride; tell yourself how great you are and remember how long you have waited for this to happen.

Sharpening perception: focus on certain elements and block out others, like closing your eyes and listening to the music.

Absorption: allow yourself to become immersed and try not to think, just sense.

Mindfulness

Two Types:
>*Formal* – Meditation
>*Informal* – Present moment attention

Imagine you read about a pill that, if taken once a day, will enhance your self-fulfillment, reduce anxiety and increase your contentment.

Would you take it?

Imagine that this pill had further positive effects such as increased self-esteem, empathy, trust and improved memory. Imagine, finally, that this pill is natural and costs you nothing.

Would you take it?

This pill exists. It's called '*meditation.*' –Haidt, 2006.

Formal mindfulness/meditation
Some physiological effects of meditation include:

- Positive impact on the cardiovascular system.
- Positive impact on blood pressure and hypertension
- Effectiveness in the treatment of disease.
- Alleviation of pain.

Behavioral, psychological and cognitive influences:
- Improved sleep.
- Improved memory and intelligence.
- Decreased anxiety and stress.
- Helps with overcoming addictions.

Meditation techniques

There are a variety of ways in which you can practice formal mindfulness (meditation). The versatility of meditation is shown in the activities below:

1. Focus on sense organs **vs** complete withdrawal from the senses.
2. Based upon mental images **vs** forbidding attention to mental images.
3. Immobility/inaction **vs** movement/walking.
4. Encouraging feelings/emotion **vs** emphasising indifference.

All the afore-mentioned meditation techniques attempt to

"Focus attention in a non-analytical way and an attempt to not dwell on discursive, ruminating thought." –Shapiro, 1982.

or meditation is *any moment when you are one with the experience.*

Informal mindfulness

Paying attention to the present moment without judgement is the essence of informal mindfulness.

It's as simple as being *in the zone* while exercising, washing the dishes, preparing dinner, or - a tricky one for most of us - listening to someone, without planning what to say next.

TIP!
I practice informal mindfulness in daily activities, including when stuck in traffic. A good method for me is to just be in the moment and focus on the things going on around me by looking out of the window. I often listen to music, focus on the details of my car interior, etc. anything to keep my mind 100% focused on the present. The fact remains I will be late… life goes on and it couldn't care less about traffic jams.

It also works well when in a shopping center queue.
I often focus on the items people have bought instead of nervously looking at my watch.

Here are eight tips to enhance daily mindfulness:

1. When you first wake up in the morning: before you get out of bed, bring your attention to your breathing. Observe five mindful breaths.

2. Notice changes in your posture: be aware of how your body and mind feel when you move from lying down to sitting, to standing, to walking. Notice each time you make a transition from one posture to the next.

3. Throughout the day: take a few moments to bring your attention to your breathing. Observe five mindful breaths.

4. Whenever you eat or drink something, take a minute and breathe: bring awareness to seeing your food, smelling your food, tasting your food, chewing your food, and swallowing your food – food for pleasure instead of energy.

5. Notice your body while you walk or stand: take a moment to notice your posture. Pay attention to the ground under your feet. Feel the air on your face, arms, and legs as you walk.

6. Bring awareness to listening and talking: can you listen without agreeing or disagreeing, liking or disliking, or planning what you will say when it is your turn?

7. Whenever you wait in a line, use this time to notice standing and breathing: feel your feet on the floor and how your body feels. Look around you without judging.

Are you feeling impatient?

8. Bring mindfulness to each activity: focus attention on daily activities such as brushing your teeth, washing up, brushing your hair, putting on your shoes, doing your job.

For people who cannot spare the thirty minutes to an hour a day to practice meditation, informal mindfulness can be a starting point. A few minutes a day of meditation and an additional few of informal mindfulness is a great path to greater acceptance and awareness.

Additional notes

Mindfulness in its formal state is not for everyone, just like ice-hockey, skydiving, marathons, etc. aren't. My curious personality and Mediterranean temperament are too active to meditate for thirty or so minutes. It's like yoga: we know it's good for us, but some of us prefer to lift weights, run, or Zumba. Stimulating experiences attract extroverts. Introverts are more drawn to introspection and meditation. Different stokes for different folks and that's the beauty of mindfulness, because you can choose informal mindfulness at any time.

Savoring

Is a conscious habit where you find yourself thinking, 'This is a great moment,' and you capture it with all your senses. We all have different responsibilities and schedules to fulfil, so savoring is just ME time. This is where you get to block all other thoughts and savor the pleasant moment/ experience in all its greatness. The more moments you savor in your life the happier you will be as you have chosen a life path worth savoring.

Live with all your senses heightened and enjoy life's fruits.

HEART OF GRATITUDE

A blind boy sat on the steps of a building with a hat by his feet. He held up a sign which said: 'I am blind, please help.' There were only a few coins in the hat.

A man was walking by. He took a few coins from his pocket and dropped them into the hat. He then took the sign, turned it around, and wrote some words. He put the sign back so that everyone who walked by would see the new words. Soon the hat began to fill up. A lot more people were giving money to the blind boy. That afternoon the man who had changed the sign came to see how things were. The boy recognized his footsteps and asked,

"Were you the one who changed my sign this morning?

What did you write?"

The man said, I only wrote the truth.

I said what you said but in a different way.

I wrote: 'Today is a beautiful day but I cannot see it.'

Both signs told people that the boy was blind. But the first sign simply said the boy was blind. The second sign told people that they were so lucky that they were not blind. Should we be surprised that the second sign was more effective?

Be thankful for what you have. Be creative. Be innovative. Think differently and positively.

"Gratitude makes sense of our past, brings peace for today, and creates a vision for tomorrow." -M. Beattie.

PASSION

"Passion is defined as a strong inclination towards an activity that people like and find important, where they invest time and energy."
-Vallerand, 2003.

What activity are you most passionate about and why? The word 'passion' is French from the Latin *'passio'*, which means suffering.

Two philosophical approaches to passion:
1. **Positive** – individuals active in their passion can achieve their highest potential –Hagel, 1770 – 1831.

2. **Negative** – passion makes people lose reason and control; people are passive, slaves to their passions, which leads to suffering –Spinoza, 1632 – 1677.

In the 1970s and 1980s passion was being researched by only one branch of psychology. The main theme was "passionate love" and it was a part of close relationships. This lasted until the year 2000 where a positive psychologist (Robert Vallerand) changed the approach of examining the passion concept.

Psychology now examines passion towards activities. Studies showed that people internalise passion in two ways. Dualistic model of passion:

1. Harmonious Passion (HP).
2. Obsessive Passion (OP).

Harmonious Passion
This comes from an autonomous internalisation of behavioural regulation. This internalisation produces a strong, but controllable, desire to engage in an activity, with a sense of volition in pursuing the activity.

The activity is accepted and integrated with all aspects of self. Due to the harmonious nature of passion, people express an openness in the activity, which evokes positive experiences.

People can engage in a passionate activity in a flexible and mindful manner. Studies have found positive relationships in harmonious passion along with flow (being in the zone) and high positivity during engagement.

Obsessive Passion
A lack of fulfilment of intrinsic needs leads to the internalisation of inter- and intra-personal pressures.

This leads to an uncontrollable excitement, which derives from the attached with contingencies (feelings of social acceptance, or self-esteem) activity.

People with an obsessive passion experience more conflicts in other life areas. They are immersed in the activity even when the surroundings suggest otherwise. Rumination (thinking about causes) about an activity one is obsessed with, is common and low positivity when prevented from engaging in it.

One of Vallerand's studies found that 85% of people could identify at least one activity they were passionate about. People spend on average 8.5 hours a week on their most passionate pursuit.

Erikson's (1959) psychosocial stage during adolescence (12-18) states it's a time to 'create and identify with self', as opposed to 'role confusion'.

In Erikson's psychosocial stage between childhood and adulthood:

Morality is learned by the child and Ethics need to be developed by the adult.

Passion vs obsession
Passions and obsessions are powerful motivators to take risks and sacrifice to achieve what we desire.

Passionate people invest in personal, professional and creative growth. They want to develop their skills or abilities and keep their passions dynamic and everlasting. Passion gives you energy and motivation to work hard while being joyful. Regardless of which passionate activity you choose, the ability to direct energy into actions helps you thrive.

Obsessive people have a weaker sense of identity because they place their sense of self into their object of obsession. Obsession is a strategy for escape and a long way away from joyful and creative passion. Self-obsession and other obsessive tendencies lead to narcissism.

The Selfie Epidemic

On March 31, 2014, a news story appeared in the Adobo Chronicles website that the American Psychiatric Association had classified selfitis as:

> *The obsessive-compulsive desire to take photos of one's self and post them on social media as, a way to make up for the lack of self-esteem and to fill a gap in intimacy.*

According to the article there are three levels of the selfitis mental disorder:

Borderline: Taking photos of one's self at least three times a day but not posting them on social media.

Acute: Taking photos of one's self at least three times a day and posting each one on social media.

Chronic: Uncontrollable urge to take photos of one's self around the clock and posting the photos on social media over six times a day.

A published study in the International Journal of Health and Addiction (Griffiths and Balakrisham, 2017) of 225 participants with an average age of twenty-one confirmed the following six underlying selfitis criteria:

Environmental enhancement: Taking selfies in-particular locations to feel good and show off to others.

Social competition: Taking selfies to get more likes on social media.

Attention-seeking: Taking selfies to gain attention from others.

Mood modification: Taking selfies to feel better.

Self-confidence: Taking selfies to feel more positive about one's self.

Subjective conformity: Taking selfies to fit in with one's social group and peers.

I am sure you know of someone who might fit in any of the afore-mentioned categories. This could be the reason for the explosion of the 'selfitis' disorder hoax story.

I know individuals that make a living from posting selfies on social networks daily as written in the contract with their marketing sponsors. I also know, as I am sure you do, other individuals who post selfies in social networks just for fun.

A quick Google search will show the substantial amount of money some Instagram influencers can earn from each sponsored photo.

Is money the cause of the selfie explosion?

or

Is it due to pure narcissism and low self-esteem?

Opinions vary depending on which end of the spectrum you are in.

TIP!
Some healthy questions that could help towards finding your passion:

1. What do you already love or like doing?
2. What are you spending time on reading?

3. What drives your decisions?

4. What subjects do you most love talking about?

5. What have you always dreamed of doing?

6. Have you identified your personality strengths?

Knowing is not doing, so start: "Living Positively."

Additional notes

A life with no passion is colourless. Managing your emotions is different to passing through life with apathy. Finding your passion is important even if you don't know what it is right now.

Remember, as we age our priorities and our passions will change too. What was fun at twenty isn't as much fun at thirty, and so on. There are multiple books on passion, recommending to either refrain or go for it. It's a matter of choice, but wouldn't you like to experience a life with a variety of harmonious passions?

A harmonious passion is something you can control. You gain new knowledge, skills, different ways of doing things, and plenty of joy in the process.

An obsessive passion controls and enslaves you. It produces constant thinking about the activity that can interfere with your daily routine.

THE BOY WHO HARNESSED THE WIND

When he was only 14 years old, William Kamkwamba dreamt up a windmill that would produce electricity for his village in Malawi. The trouble? As Malawi was experiencing the worst famine in 50 years, William had to drop out of school because his family could no longer afford the $80 annual tuition.

This meant he not only had no money to purchase the parts but also no formal education to teach him how to put them together. Determined, he headed to the local library and devoured its limited selection of textbooks, then gathered scrap parts — a bicycle dynamo, bamboo poles, a tractor fan, rubber belts, a bike chain ring — and brought his vision to life, building a functioning windmill. He spent the next five years perfecting the design and founded the Moving Windmills Project in 2008 to foster rural economic development and education projects in Malawi.

"Nothing is as important as passion. No matter what you want to do in life, be passionate." -Jon Bon Jovi.

CHAPTER 11

THE GOOD LIFE (HEDONIC AND EUDEMONIC HAPPINESS)

The Good Life Equals Happiness. What is happiness? What brings happiness to our lives? Happiness is a subjective and fleeting feeling.

I would like to try and answer these questions, by addressing them through ancient wisdom.

One way to do that is to look at the differences between two well-known ancient Greek philosophies of the Good Life: *Hedonic and Eudemonic Happiness.*

Hedonic Happiness

"The art of life means enjoying pleasures as they pass. The most tempting pleasures are neither intellectual nor are they always moral." –Aristippus (435-356 BC).

Hedonic happiness as a life philosophy began in ancient Greece with Aristippus, who was a pupil of Socrates.

Through questioning the goal of human actions and what value is, for its own sake, "pleasure" was identified. Many thought of Aristippus as a pure hedonist.

In hedonic happiness, sensual gratification from delicious food, good wine, quality sleep, joyful sex, etc. (all subjective) is something to be enjoyed in the moment and not be deferred for a later time. The Greeks believed Aristippus was a slave to pleasure, due to his controversial beliefs.

When Aristippus was criticised for sleeping with a courtesan (prostitute), he asked whether there was any difference between sailing on a ship on which many people had sailed, to one which no one has sailed.

Aristippus portrayed himself as a man who could do anything for the sake of pleasure, making him flexible and liberated. The only prerequisite was to be clear-headed and single-minded when pursuing pleasure, so as not to lose self-control.

However, Aristippus was also criticised when he left his infant son to die as if he was not his own. His reply was:

"Phlegm and vermin are also of our own begetting, but we still cast them as far away from us as possible because they are useless."

British philosopher Jeremy Bentham (1748-1832) stated that: "Everyone is a hedonist, whether they believe it or not."

Philosophy views Bentham as the founder of utilitarianism (best action that maximises utility).

Bentham insisted that:

"All humans do whatever they think will give them pleasure. The dilemma of choosing pleasure or choosing health is resolved by deciding which of the two will bring you more pleasure."

For example:
1. When you choose to eat an ice-cream, it's because you think it will make you happy.
2. When you choose to eat fruit instead, it's because you think it will make you happy.

Psychology calls this "psychological hedonism."

So, are we confusing happiness with pleasure?

Pleasure is a too broad and subjective theme just like happiness. So, Bentham's pleasure equals happiness argument is viewed as a theory based on semantics (the meaning of words).

Today's common view of hedonism is:
A person who tries to maximise pleasure and minimise pain.

What's wrong with that, you might say?

Let's look at an example of extreme hedonism in the renowned Leonardo DiCaprio movie "Wolf of Wall Street." The film was based on the real-life story of Jordan Belfort; a self-made millionaire and pure hedonist, who indulged in many varieties of pleasure.

Pleasure has many types of different stimulus ranging from just thinking about previous pleasant experiences to enjoying an active sex life.

For example:

Drinking a cold beer on a sunny day, enjoying a glass of wine with its protective antioxidant flavonoids, charged training sessions in the gym - are all subjective pleasures.

Measure on the Pleasure
As with all things in life, knowing when to stop is crucial to reaping only joys from hedonic pleasures. Hedonic pleasures primarily come from the five senses: sight, sound, taste, touch and smell.

Becoming dependent on any vice, such as over-drinking, over-eating, over-exercising, is when pleasure becomes a problem. When pleasure is a yearning, an unstoppable hunger, which deprives you of other parts of your life, you are in trouble.

Rational Hedonism

Maximizing everyday pleasures while living a balanced life. Enjoying a morning cup of tea, coffee, mindful eating, or sipping a favorite beverage, is *savoring.* Along with other states, or activities, savoring links pleasure with reducing stress and inducing broader and more creative thinking. Pleasurable events have shown to put people in an optimistic mood, which benefits overall well-being. RECAP: Hedonic (Subjective Wellbeing)

- Presence of positive mood
- Absence of negative mood
- Satisfaction with various life domains
- Global life satisfaction

Eudemonic Happiness

Aristotle (384 – 322 BC) coined the concept eudemonia (demon – true nature) and along with Plato is considered, to be the father of Western philosophy.

Aristotle was a student of Plato, founder of Lyceum and tutor of Alexander the Great (356 – 323 BC). He asks:

Can someone be truly fulfilled without knowing what he or she is living for?

What is the point?

What is the meaning of one's existence?

The demon in action looks at the development possibilities each person has at their disposal. Realizing your full potential, working on ethics, or living according to your virtues is the true path to well-being and happiness.
In all corners of the earth, people are seeking pleasure, wealth, status and a good reputation. Aristotle questions the real value of most pleasure-seeking hedonic acts.
The Greek philosopher stated: *"We desire pleasure, money, success, etc. for one main reason **"to be happy"**, or at the very least, the idea that certain actions/states will bring happiness to our lives."*

Through observing nature Aristotle argued that:

Vegetative life: plants and wilderness need nourishment from sunshine and water for growth.

Animals: animals seek pleasure, and reproduction. A happy looking pet is thought of as a healthy companion.

Humans: Only humans can reason and act according to their principles and, therefore, can take responsibility for their own actions.

So, where is the balance between the two distinct

philosophical approaches to happiness of Hedonia and Eudemonia?

Psychologist Waterman (1993) developed the Personally Expressive Activities Questionnaire (PEAQ) to investigate hedonic and eudemonic pleasures while people were engaged in activities.

The studies showed that people experience far less eudemonic experiences than hedonic experiences through the five senses of taste, touch, smell, hearing and sight. Both pursuits of happiness were correlated with positive thinking affects.

Difference in feelings/states when engaging in activities:
Hedonic happiness - relaxed, excited, content, happy, losing track of time and forgetting personal problems.
Eudemonic happiness - invest effort, have clear goals, assertiveness, challenged, high concentration levels.

RECAP: Eudemonic (Psychological Wellbeing)
- Sense of control or autonomy
- Feeling of meaning and purpose
- Personal expressiveness
- Feelings of belonging
- Social contribution
- Competence
- Personal growth
- Self-acceptance

Conclusion

Hedonia is about pleasure.

Eudemonia gives you the opportunity to advance your personal potential, in skills, talents and life purpose. However, both philosophies of the good life are subjective. Living a life with a balanced engagement of hedonic and eudemonic activities/states promotes overall well-being.

Additional notes

The Good Life is attractive for every human and, by using our five senses, we can attain hedonia if only for a while. If our senses are stimulated constantly it would only be a matter of time before we overdosed on pleasure. Looking forward to the weekend or a planned trip, reserving a table for dinner, watching or playing sports, engaging in enjoyable activities and hobbies, etc. are all sensual pleasures. A person who has few pleasures is depriving themselves of joy.

Along with hedonic satisfaction, which, if misused, can lead to several addictions, we are so much more than just our senses. An internal yearning for cognitive, spiritual, intuitive meaning is necessary for the soul. It is our well-being, a guide of where we are heading in life and how we are doing so far.

The number of addictions, abuses, and self-harming practices are rising. It could be due to people's lack of understanding in the importance of spending some of their resourses and precious time in developing their inner-self. There are many sources available on the internet with valuable tips. Practical information on nourishing your inner-being and identifying your own meaning of life is essential.

THE WISE MAN

Visitors to a wise man complained about the same problems over-and-over again. One day, he decided to tell them a joke and they all roared with laughter.

After a few minutes, he told them the same joke and only a few of them smiled.

Then he told the same joke for a third time, but no one laughed or smiled anymore. The wise man smiled and said: "You can't laugh at the same joke over and over. So why are you always crying about the same problem?"

Moral of the story: Worrying won't solve your problems, it'll just waste your time and energy. Enjoy the fruits you already have and make your own interpretation of the good life.

"My mission in life is not merely to survive, but to thrive; and to do so with some passion, some compassion, some humor and some style." -Maya Angelou.

CHAPTER 12

PERMA

A founding father of Positive Psychology, Martin Seligman believes that the PERMA model is essential to well-being. It started in 1998 when Dr Seligman was president of the American Psychological Association. After decades of involvement with mental disorders, Seligman decided that the psychological focus must switch from what was wrong with people to what was right with them.

During many years of scientific research on happiness, Seligman identified five building blocks of well-being. The essential elements make up the acronym PERMA.

- Positive emotions
- Engagement
- Relationships
- Meaning
- Accomplishment

Positive Emotions

What do you say when asked if you are satisfied with your life?

If I were to take an educated guess, the answer depends on your mood at the time of asking.

When in a positive state:
The past makes you feel 'grateful'.

The present is one you 'appreciate'.

The future is filled with 'hope'.

The reason is that good feelings not only put a smile on your face, but inspire you to be more creative and productive at work. You also perform better in other activities, enhance your immune system and put a spring in your step.

CAUTION!
Positive emotions and feeling good are contagious!
To test this theory, sit close to someone you know well.
Then place your face a few centimeters away from theirs.

Now I would like you to tell them to keep a straight face. And for the next two minutes, smile at them with all your heart.

I bet even the stiffest, toughest, most conservative and reserved person you try this experiment on will buckle and smile back at you (do not try this with strangers).

If you are unsuccessful, feel free to email me about the results, as in all my research I haven't come across a non-smiling face yet.

Back to positive emotions….
A life without going through periods of loss is not realistic. The important lesson to take from the not great moments of our lives is to not dwell on the negativity.

Repetitive thinking of doom and gloom is the way to depression.

Along with feelings of anxiety regarding future concerns there is also a danger of becoming pessimistic in all areas of life. This is the exact opposite effect of when we feel positive emotions.

Recognition of our positive emotions is crucial to our ability to sustain a joyful present and hopeful future.

TIP!
Engaging in:
- activities that make you feel good
- spending time with loved ones and friends
- working out in the gym

- exercising or swimming
- eating or cooking tasty food
- enjoying nature, hiking
- spending time on our hobbies
- dancing, singing, playing music
- trying a new activity

are ways you can experience positive emotions.

The upward spiral of positive emotions entails:
Contentment – Hopefulness – Optimism – Positive Expectations – Enthusiasm – Passion – **JOY.**

The downward spiral of negative emotions entails:
Boredom – Pessimism – Irritation – Disappointment – Doubt – Worry – Anger – Hatred – Jealousy – Insecurity – **FEAR.**

Barbara Fredrickson (2001) is an expert in positive emotions and she encourages us to use positive emotions in-order to "broaden and build."

The 'broaden and build' theory has shown to lead to new positive behaviours that help people strengthen relationships and become more resilient.

Positive feelings help us live in the moment: *"Carpe diem."*

> *"The best way to overcome undesirable or negative thoughts and feelings is to cultivate the positive ones."*
> -William Atkinson.

Engagement

Life without developing and being absorbed in personal and professional activities leads to boredom and feelings of uselessness.

Mihaly Csikszentmihayli (1975), coined the term *flow* and is also one of the three founding fathers of positive psychology. The other two founding fathers of modern positive psychology are Martin Seligman and Christopher Peterson.

Csikszentmihayli's research focused on understanding the timeline of when people are more creative, productive and often happiest. He conducted many interviews on athletes, musicians, artists, etc. as they are groups that experienced the most optimal performance levels.

The research showed that flow was essential to create happiness and that: *Happiness takes a committed effort to be manifested.*

The eight characteristics of flow:

1. Complete concentration on the task.
2. Clarity of goals and reward in mind and immediate feedback.

3. Transformation of time (speeding up/slowing down of time).

4. The experience is intrinsically rewarding, has an end in-itself.

5. Effortlessness and ease.

6. There is a balance between challenge and skills.

7. Actions and awareness are merged, losing self-conscious rumination.

8. There is a feeling of control over the task.

People with high interest in life and persistence *(autotelic personalities)* are more likely to master challenging tasks, which are important characteristics for flow experience. However, the challenges must not be bigger than one's level of skills, nor the skill be too much for the size of the challenge.

Inducing flow is about the balance between the level of skill and the size of the challenge at hand.

The essence of engagement in a word is momentum. Imagine it's a cold and wet Monday morning and you are tucked in under a warm duvet. Just thinking about getting out of bed will get you nowhere. Now imagine what happens when you are jogging. Because you are in motion, there is no time to think, so you're doing it, as one foot goes in front of the other. You are absorbed in the moment. This engagement can be felt in any activity such cooking, baking, painting, dancing, etc.

Becoming absorbed in daily activities, especially if you are fortunate enough to enjoy your work, means you are more likely to reach your full potential.

Positive psychology identifies and cultivates personal strengths and talents. Once you identify your strengths, conscious engagement follows, resulting in a boost of all-round confidence.

You can also use informal mindfulness to enhance your clear awareness in the present, both mentally and physically.

Relationships

The strong need for connection with others defines humans as social animals, hence the saying:

> "Happiness shared is happiness squared."

Sharing feelings of joy with people we care about provides us with even more joy. The personal connections with significant others can help maintain balance in our lives. Loneliness can become an unbearable feeling, which can bring on various psychological and physiological disorders. Being a member of a community or group widens your net of human support. In multiple studies of happiness, relationships are always at the top. The eighty-year, Harvard graduate study, which started in 1938 and is still ongoing, is convincing research indicating relationships as crucial to happiness.

We make positive relationships when we rely on others for care, love, laughter, boosts of confidence, a shoulder to cry on, etc. It's a two-way process, where hearing with your eyes and talking with your heart works well.

Tuning in to another person's body language signals and picking up cues of high tension on emotional-feelings is valued in relationships.

Trusting and sharing creates a deep empathy in relationships as nothing can strengthen a bond more than reliability and support. However, these are things that take time to develop.

Saying that, there might come a time when just a brief encounter with someone could feel like you've known them for ages.

Having the same values and showing gratitude for the people in our lives builds strong and positive relationships.

"The meeting of two personalities is like the contact of two chemical substances: if there is any reaction, both are transformed." –Carl Jung.

Meaning

We are all terrified of boredom.

The avoidance of boredom is a strong reason for why we should choose a life of meaning and purpose. Being minimally satisfied with our lives, at work, with loved ones, friends, or activities, is difficult if we are not engaged. Contentment is a feeling of deep satisfaction that comes when meaning is driving your life. Our self-worth relates to the tasks we participate in daily. Finding joy in our activities works well when we are working to the best of our talents and skills.

"People's lives usually draw meaning from multiple sources, including family and love, work, religion, and various personal projects."
-Robert Emmons.

Researchers Baumeister and Vohs (2005), associate the quest for finding meaning in life with four core needs:

1. **Purpose:** present events draw meaning from their connection to future outcomes — objective goals and subjective fulfilment.
2. **Values:** which can justify certain courses of action.
3. **Efficacy:** the belief that one can make a difference.
4. **Self-worth:** reasons for believing one is a good and worthy person results from immersion in our natural talents or what we excel at.

What do you value most in this world?

Once you have identified what you feel strongly about e.g. family, faith, love of learning, helping mentally or physically challenged people, etc., find like-minded people and work together towards the things you care about.

Finding meaning in our personal and professional lives provides us with a true purpose, which leads to a fulfilling life.

Accomplishment

A life without goals or ambition can lead to apathy. Setting realistic targets and achieving them gives us a sense of satisfaction and fulfilment. Yet people tell us throughout our lives that winning isn't important.

Striving for success is important, but the journey rather than the prize might be more significant to our well-being. However, to achieve happiness we need wins.

What is the point of setting goals if we never achieve them? When looking back at your life it is important to have experienced a sense of accomplishment. Our previous successes, regardless of their size, add to our overall self-confidence. This belief makes us feel more optimistic and hopeful about future attempts.

Previous psychological circles viewed feelings of pride as a selfish behaviour. However, contemporary psychology interprets having pride in one's own accomplishments (provided they were moral), a self-esteem boost.

When you feel good about yourself there is a high probability you will share your knowledge and expertise with others.

Apart from motivating yourself to achieve success through harder and smarter work, you may even inspire other people to work on their goals.

The dopamine rush we get when achieving a goal is short-lived and insufficient to produce a lasting good mood, or behaviour. Many lottery winners reverted to their baseline temperament levels after the initial spike of accomplishment.

In contrast, people who win goals, awards, races, competitions, etc. are driven more by their efforts than the result. Knowledge of your own capabilities brings you a continuous satisfaction in life as it drives you to accomplish whatever you set out to do.

Building up tolerance to rejections or losses can fortify you with the will to keep striving until you succeed. Many people believe luck is the main reason for success. I will not argue that this isn't true sometimes, but often, continuous effort and persistence results in luck.

"I'm a great believer in luck and find that the harder I work that more I have of it." -Thomas Jefferson.

Additional notes

PERMA is positive psychology's interpretation of the good life. It's a scientific guide on how to live a life with strategies that are logical and practical. The focus on looking at what was wrong with people frustrated Seligman, so he shifted his attention to what was right with people. Knowing what you do well and what gives you joy, provides you with the will to move forward with confidence.

CHAPTER 13

LIFE IS PLEASURE

The pleasure principle. Sigmund Freud (1856 – 1939) coined the phrase 'pleasure principle' when he described people as either wanting to *"seek pleasure or avoid pain."*

Regarding avoiding pain, people will go to great lengths to avoid even momentary pain. Dentist and surgeon appointments are not on many people's desirable to do lists. Psychoanalytic theory proposes the **id** *(0-3years old)* is part of the unconscious dedicated to pleasure. This is visible in infants where immediate gratification is their primary purpose. It comprises primitive urges of hunger, thirst, anger, etc.

Psychoanalysts believe the **id**, is one of the strongest motivators, at the deepest unconscious level. Later in life as children, we learn to delay gratification and become more realistic about the future.

Only when the **ego** (3-5years old) develops, we learn not to grab others ice-cream, but instead ask if we can have some.

Can you imagine what would happen if you took your boss's sandwich out of their hand because you were hungry?

During the phallic stage of development from five years old onwards the **superego**, or moral side grows.

Some like to call the superego the conscious right or wrong part of our psyche.

Tony Robbins (1991), a successful life coach, believes there are two types of people – those who seek pleasure and those that avoid pain.

Think about it for a minute.

Looking back at your life so far:

Are you a person who looks for pleasure often?

or

Do you refrain, or limit pleasure opportunities?

How about this principle?
Why do we take-action? To seek pleasure.

Why do we procrastinate? Because an action might cause pain or rejection.

We will do anything possible to avoid pain. It is programmed into our psyche. Life teaches many people to focus on avoiding pain rather than to seek pleasure.
We rarely change much during our lifetime, because our internal links to pain or pleasure don't change, hence the quote 'a leopard can't change its spots.'

All marketing targets our pleasure principles with their products. However, people separate successes and failures in life according to their values and beliefs.

If you could only pick *one* of the following states, which would you choose?

- Security
- Love
- Adventure
- Comfort or Success

Different people choose different things, which are all linked to their values.

Two types of Values
Moving towards values – love, attraction, success, or states that create pleasure.

Moving away from values – anger, pain, depression, or states you avoid.

People's lifestyles are created, shaped and lived according to values they want or fear most.

For instance, say you want to be successful, but you fear rejection. Your chances of success are limited by your fear or avoiding pain/rejection. The way you live your life is highly influenced by your childhood. You learned to seek pleasure or avoid pain from your parents or caregivers. The beliefs or rules are your internal guide of what must happen in-order to feel successful or fulfilled.

However, success can be achieved, but it is not the same thing as 'fulfilment'.

Being fulfilled is far greater for your well-being than success!

A person can be successful in their professional field, yet feel unfulfilled in their personal life and vice versa. Even though it's a constant process, beliefs and values can change if we feel unfulfilled about where life is taking us. That's when we think: *it's time to change my career, relationship status, residence, country, lifestyle, etc.*

It starts with an internal conflict and a strong desire to change certain aspects of our life.

The mid-life crisis global phenomenon is a common occurrence for a few reasons. Psychologists link a big part of the depression that sets in in our forties with a feeling of lack of accomplishment or fulfilment.

In our contemporary society, there are many professionals to help guide you through change.

In the *Good Greek Life*, Socrates believed reason was the path to the good life.

Philosophy convinced Socrates about the power of introspection and he declared that "the unexamined life is not worth living."

People could achieve desires along with happiness only if they put in an effort as mere mortals in ancient Greece. Plato wrote about the pursuits of pleasure and happiness:

> *"All human being and happiness depends on learning to harmonize our desires. Knowledge and virtue is more important than physical desires."*

Modern Psychology's often used term *"it's all relative"* was probably coined by Socrates.

Socrates believed all pleasure is relative. For instance, the relief you get after getting over a common cold.

Breathing is pleasure....

How often do we stop to think of breathing as pleasure?

Finding a nice corner office job after working on a production line is pleasure….

How long will the pleasurable effect of the corner office last?

We also derive pleasure from taking drugs… How short is the period of pleasure and how long is the term of some drug related addictions?

Epicurus believed in positive and negative pleasures.

"The removal of any kind of pain is a positive pleasure".

For instance, the simple quench of thirst from drinking a glass of water on a hot day is a positive pleasure. Negative pleasure is when you require nothing to feel pleasure, you are in a state of not wanting.

According to Epicurus, the absence of unfulfilled desires is the true state of happiness, a similar concept to the Buddhist principle of Nirvana.

Aristotle proposed that pleasure is found in many activities such as thinking, music, art, or hobbies. The better an individual becomes in their choice of activity the higher the state of pleasure.

Contemporary thinkers believe in guilt-free pleasures. Positivity and generosity provide us with internal/thinking pleasure and the Italian cliché:

"Move forward and let others do the same."

From a neurobiological perspective of pleasure, we've known for a long time that human brains are hard-wired to seek pleasure. Research has shown that a steady supply of healthy pleasure and satisfaction is crucial to a life of quality and well-being.

Healthy behaviors, from various hobbies to eating fresh produce, cooking exotic food, etc., are good for us. The pleasure-seeking unhealthy behaviors of taking drugs, abusing alcohol and overeating can be detrimental to our health.

The reward pathways and reward centers in our brain are stimulated by pleasurable activities from sensitive touch, pleasant music, good flavor, nice aromas and interesting sights. The release of chemical neurotransmitters during the pleasurable physical events also lead to positive emotion.

Kenneth Blum (1996), suggests that if we don't have enough healthy resources of pleasure in our lives a "reward deficiency" can trigger self-comforting through harmful addictions, cravings and compulsions.

The left prefrontal cortex (brain center of happiness) creates positive emotions. A variety of endorphins released after pleasure signals, hook up to opioid receptors and result in feelings of well-being and bliss (runner's high).

Two Types of pleasure varieties

Feel good pleasure – sensations: delicious food, feel of silk, massages, beautiful images, art, music, etc. The soothing effects of touching we receive from oxytocin induces general overall growth and increases healing and bonding.

Value based pleasure – meaningful: accomplishing important goals, committing or connecting with things of importance. Goals developed slowly endure and give us a sense of meaning and internal calmness.

Ask yourself:
- What is the purpose of life without pleasure?
- What is the purpose of money?
- What is the point of seeking a job you like?
- Why look for a lovable partner?
- Why start a family?
- Why buy a house with a garden, a fast car? Why swim in blue seas, etc.
- You can see where I am going with this…
- Once all is said and done, you and only you have a choice to live a life of pleasure while limiting the possibility of pain for yourself, or others in the present, near and distant future.

- Pain results from abusing pleasures of flesh, drink, food, drugs, psychological stress and damaging habits.
- You cannot choose the family you are born in, or your upbringing.
- You cannot choose your innate genetic predispositions or abilities.
- You cannot choose your birth sex, skin color or race.
- You cannot choose a privileged private, or elite education.

TIP!

What you can choose is:

- To live with a lot of zest and vigor for life.
- To take care of your body, mind and soul.
- To celebrate life daily.
- To live with purpose and meaning.
- To give yourself frequent pats on the back.
- To choose a healthy and fulfilling lifestyle.
- To show your loved ones you care about them.
- To treat yourself as the unique person you are.
- **Choose a life of meaning and pleasure!**

Additional notes

Pleasure is necessary and so are the borders that define it. The media is full of privileged celebrities and sports icons who have lost control of their pleasures.

Be it sex addiction, food addiction, compulsive surfing on the internet, to using recreational drugs, instead of choosing the pleasure, it chooses you.

I like chocolate and ice-cream as many others do, but I also know that too much can lead to insulin problems, sugar crashes, and body image issues.

Experiencing a variety of fruits is the essence of life. We were born to enjoy the pleasures available to us along with a brain that seeks them. By developing our emotional intelligence, we gain control of harmful urges.

Control rewards us with many positives without the negative side-effects.

THE PLEASURE OF FREEDOM

Once, in a jungle, a beautiful golden bird had made her home in a tree. When she sang, shiny pearls fell from her open beak.

One day a bird catcher came to the jungle. Soon he spread a net and the poor golden bird was caught in it. The bird catcher took the bird home and kept it in a silver cage and fed it well. But the sad bird did not sing at all and the hunter never got any pearls.

The bird catcher sold the caged bird to a merchant. The merchant gifted that golden bird to the king. The king thought, "Hmm ... that's a nice bird. I'll give it to the princess to play with."

So, the king gave the caged bird to the princess.
She was a beautiful girl with a kind heart.

She at once freed the golden bird. The pleasure of freedom made the golden bird sing aloud and soon a shower of pearls fell.

The golden bird came to meet the princess every day and sang for her.

"Simply enjoy life and the great pleasures that come with it." -Karolina Kurkova.

MOTIVATION

"Why don't we do what's best for us?
Why do we abandon good decisions for bad?
Why can't we follow through ideas and plans?
Why do we procrastinate so often?" –Plato (428-348 BC).

Is it laziness? Ancient Greek philosophers coined the term "akrasia", which describes a state of acting against one's better judgement, or a lack of will that prevents us from doing the right thing.

American philosopher David Donaldson (2001), views akrasia as a natural process which occurs when we exchange a long-term goal for immediate available pleasure, i.e. watching TV, eating a snack, using social media, etc.

Motivation theories are popular if we judge by the plethora of books, videos and how-to guides that are available.

Instinct Theory - In the 1870s Wilhelm Wundt coined the term 'instinct' to refer to repeated behavior. The instinctual innate tendencies of behaving in certain unlearned patterns such as dogs shaking when wet, or mothers taking care of their children supports the instinct theory. However, the instinct theory of motivation fails to explain why people exhibit different levels of jealousy and aggression, and the lack of maternal care in some women.

Drive Reduction Theory – In 1943 Clark Hull developed the first theory of motivation (drive reduction theory). He based the principle on the idea that all motivation arises because of the need to fulfil certain needs. Hunger, thirst, and sex are examples of primary drives, and we are conditioned to have other drives such as money. Hull believed reinforcement and conditioning to explain behavior. However, if 'homeostasis" (a state of balance) was enough, seeking excitement would not be a common human need. Money itself does not fulfil a biological or psychological need. The drive reduction principle in motivation theory fails to explain the deliberate intensity seeking behavior of humans and animals.

Arousal Theory – In 1908 Robert Yerkes and John Dodson proposed that performance and arousal are directly related. The Yerkes-Dodson Law, which is still in use today and is a principle of arousal theory, states that increased levels of arousal will improve performance, but only until optimal levels are reached. People seek their own stimulation to maintain optimal arousal levels. If you're tired or anxious your performance level will suffer. The ideal state is between low and intense levels of arousal and these vary from person to person. Finding your subjective level of optimal arousal will enhance performance in any task you undertake, thus making it more enjoyable.

Incentive Theory – Incentives theories started back in the 1940s and 1950s. The theory proposed that motivation is based on the pull of external goals (money, rewards, status). Marketing campaigns work on that same principle of making you want something and thinking you will be better off once you possess it. Incentive theory suggests that our actions are influenced by outside incentives. The psychology of selling uses this theory in shops, where an expensive item is strategically placed near the cashier's till. The impulse to buy is enhanced by thinking you deserve a treat after practicing self-restraint with other purchases. This is called "ego depletion".

Self-Actualization Theory – Abraham Maslow proposed in 1943 a hierarchy of human needs. The theory outlines a progressive movement towards self-actualization. The stages are:

1. Physiological needs
2. Safety
3. Love and Belonging
4. Self-esteem
5. Self-actualization.

Stage 5 occurs in later years in life and only for a few-accomplished intellectuals. Only by pursuing and achieving your full potential will you be satisfied. The problem is that some people might not satisfy their lower needs before moving on to higher ones.

Apart from some well-known figures in history, which Maslow believed were self-actualized, the general message is to focus on our own meaning of reaching "greatness."

Cognitive Theory – Ed Deci and Richard Ryan (1985), propose that it is expectation that drives our behavior. They divide this theory into *intrinsic motivation and extrinsic motivation.* Intrinsic motivation deals with inner interests where you can express your true-self at work or leisure. You are in control of the outcome as you choose the behavior and effort in every task, expecting an appropriate outcome. Extrinsic motivation involves rewards like money, status, prestige, sports cars, luxury and recognition. Wanting or desiring more could lead to "motivational crowding out," so you stop doing what you enjoy and become enslaved to extrinsic desires.

Self- Determination Theory

Deci and Ryan (2000), updated their original Cognitive theory of motivation and introduced Self-Determination Theory **(SDT).**

There are still two basic types of motivation…

Intrinsic and Extrinsic motivation

Intrinsic - starts from within and can vary from personal goal values, to the highest intrinsic motivation of wanting to do them.

Extrinsic - performed in-order to reap positive external rewards or to avoid punishment.

Examples:

Intrinsic motivation

You pick up a book which you find interesting to read. The motivation to finish it is intrinsic and easy to find. You can repeat this process throughout life with the same degree of intrinsic motivation each time you find an interesting book to read.

Extrinsic motivation

You pick up a book to read just to pass an exam, so the motivation is extrinsic, and the process can become boring. This process can be repeated throughout life with the same lack of enthusiasm.

Sometimes in life we must grind our teeth and get on with it. The emphasis is on the frequency we put ourselves through hard enduring tasks for extrinsic purposes. Owning large houses, sports cars, designer clothes, travelling to exotic places are joyful for many people. But at what cost?

We could correlate the decline of happiness in rich countries, such as the U.S.A. and the U.K, which are well known for their consuming and materialistic lifestyles, to pure extrinsic motivation.

Some parents struggle throughout their lives to give their children a better future (financial) without realizing the negative consequences it might have both on themselves and their offspring.

There is no guarantee that children will appreciate their parents' efforts for a prosperous future.

If this was the case, rehab centers in wealthy countries wouldn't be filled with rich clients wanting to gain back control over their pleasures.

Teaching the young generation by showing them how to live with intrinsic motivation is more important than chasing a promotion.

If a higher salary means spending money on buying more gadgets or designer clothing, it will induce greedy behavior. Participate in intrinsic motivational activities. You only get one life to live as you choose, by your rules.

However, in some professions, where the love of the work is important, long periods of hard studying are required, such as in medicine, law, architecture, etc.

Wouldn't life be great if we pursued motivating tasks, which are enjoyable, long lasting and self- fulfilling?

Self Determination Theory grew in the 1980s, due to its focus on three intrinsic motivational needs. According to Ryan and Deci, these three basic needs are necessary for growth and fulfilment, which are every human's goal. *Competence* – The desire to control and master the environment and outcome. Experiencing mastery and wanting to know how things will turn out and seeing the results of our actions are satisfying.

Relatedness – The desire to interact, be connected to, and experience caring for other people. During our daily activities and actions with other people we seek the wholesome feeling of belonging.

Autonomy – The universal urge to act in harmony with one's integrated self; it does not mean independent of others. It means having a sense of free will when doing something or acting out of our own interests and values.

A typical person who leads a life of high self-determination, high thinking and acting, is autonomous, intrinsically motivated, and is best described as someone who believes they control their own life. They will:

Take responsibility for their own behavior, good or bad.
Be self-motivated and not driven by others' standards.

Determine their actions based on own internal values. Every action they take has motivation behind it.

In your own life, for example, did you maybe take up golf because you enjoy it? Or was it because you see it as prestigious and something that will provide networking opportunities?

Do we do things because we enjoy them? Or to impress others?

*"Control your own destiny or someone else will." –*Jack Wells.

Four additional motivational trait theories:

Motivational Traits 1

***Towards goals (40%)** = Focused on goals and achievement.*
Attain
Obtain
Have
Get
Include

***Away (40%)** = Recognize what should be avoided*
Avoid
Steer clear of
Not have
Get rid of
Exclude

What is important about recognition and independence for you?

I'd be free to see the world
vs
Don't want to depend on borrowed finances.

Motivational Traits 2

Internal motivation (40%) *= Provide own motivation, decide on quality of own work.*
Only I can decide
It's up to me
I'll consider that

External (40%) *= Need other people's opinions and outside direction.*
They think…
The feedback I got
They noticed

How will you know you have achieved your goal?

I'll feel good about it
vs
People will tell me they are impressed.

Motivational Traits 3

Procedures (40%) *= Likes to follow a set process - believes there is a right way to do things.*

First…then…after which

The right way

Tried and tested

Options (40%) *= Likes opportunities, possibilities to do it differently.*

Opportunity

Choices, Alternatives

Expanding, possibilities

What will be your approach to achieving your goal?

Write a plan, get a coach, create action lists

vs

try stuff out, find out what works.

Motivational Traits 4

Proactive (15-20%) = Initiate, jump in, bulldoze

Do it

Go for it

Get it done

Don't wait

Reactive (15-20%) = Wait, consider. analyze.

Understand

Think about it

Might

Could

Where will you get support to achieve your success?

I will find the support I need by networking

vs

The right people will find me.

Additional notes

Motivation theories are about igniting the human spirit. Many books focus on stopping procrastination.

I believe in setting a goal or having something substantial to aim for. Our subconscious can't understand the word *don't*. This is common in procrastination, hence the difficulty in motivating yourself for long-lasting change.

In many psychological circles the term: *self-fulfilling prophecy*, is used. This means you usually get what you think about. The science of applied positive psychology moves a step further by encouraging people to take-action.

Taking-action is the only way to progress towards fulfilment. Motivation is healthier when intrinsic, as in self-determination theory. But please remember to enjoy extrinsic pleasure along the way.

Self-determination theory has shown a high rate of success in motivating employees. One positive is the trickle-down effect in personal contexts too. After all, who doesn't want to live a life feeling competent, autonomous and with relatedness?

"All our dreams can come true, if we have the courage to pursue them." -Walt Disney.

C H A P T E R 1 5
RESILIENCE

"Do not judge me by my success, judge me by how many times I fell down and got back up again." -Ernest Hemingway.

When faced with adversity in life: How do you cope or adapt? Why do some people bounce back quicker than others? Why do some people get stuck in life? When faced with a tragedy, natural disaster, health problem, relationship trouble, work issue, or school matter, a person's resilience will determine how well they will adapt.

A person with a healthy amount of resilience can bounce back quicker than someone whose resilience is less developed.

"If you can't change it, change the way you think about it."
- Mary Engelbreit.

What is the foundation of resilience?
Resilience is a characteristic strength, which starts at a

young age and is heavily influenced by parenting style. The most resilient children are those raised with an *authoritative* parenting style, as opposed to authoritarian, permissive, or uninvolved.

Authoritative Parenting
Effort in creating and maintaining a positive relationship. Explaining the reasons behind the rules.

Enforcing rules and giving consequences while considering the child's feelings.

Thinking back to my childhood, I can say that my grandparents could have been a little more authoritative. I had a shock at the age of twelve when I discovered that I was not the favorite child anymore.

It was my two-years older step-sister in London. She was given more pocket money and was called a princess.

Quite a difficult circumstance for me as I was used to being spoiled.

While I was living in Greece, my two years' younger sister had to do everything around the house. I was the firstborn bearing my grandad's name, so being treated as special seemed normal.

I remember at age six, refusing to eat a boiled egg unless

my granny gave it to me on top of the wardrobe. No wonder I grew up with insecurity issues, including often crying after naps.

Looking back, my sister did everything for me. Often, she walked to the grocery store during hot summer afternoons just to get me grapes.

Being treated as second best might not seem adverse, you might think. My resilience kicked in at eighteen, when my dad emigrated to Canada with his much-younger fourth wife. This was a period where I was pursuing a business education, acting and singing.

Reality was like a knockout punch when my dad told me that from now on I had to take care of myself.

The icing on the cake was that he sold the family house I was living in and left me with very little money.

The days of driving to college carefree were long gone and the immediate goal for me now was to find a safe place to stay. Income was also a crucial factor as life in London, even in the eighties, was not cheap.

I swallowed my pride and found a bedsit in a shady part of North London where the rent was low. I knew there and then that regardless of my limited square meter space that I had to make this room my headquarters.

Triple locking the door was normal in the neighbour-hood and after a while it became second nature. Keeping myself to myself was an integral part of staying safe, while hoping that one day I'd move out.

Was I scared?
Did I have doubts?
Did I question my resilience?
Yes, to all the above.

Did I ever think of giving up?
Did I think of going back to Greece?
Did I ever show any weakness?
No, to all the above.

Was this the only time my resilience helped me overcome living alone in London with little money and no family?
Not by far.

I've encountered multiple challenging situations, where only sheer resilience kept me believing that through every dark night, there's a bright day that follows.

Resilience in Children

In 1955 Werner and Smith began a longitudinal study that followed children born on the Hawaiian island of Kauai. Mental health workers, nurses and pediatricians monitored the 698 multi-racial children through a 40-year life span.

Thirty percent of the participants were born and raised in poverty and troubled families. Some negative circumstances included parental psychopathology, alcoholism, divorce and mothers with less than eight years' education.

Two-thirds of the children who had experienced four or more risk factors developed learning problems by age 2, behavioral problems by age 10, and mental problems by age 18. However, one out of three high-risk group children grew into competent, caring and confident adults. They went on to be successful in school, led healthy social lives and were all employed at age forty.

So, what stopped these children developing social issues? The researchers identified *three* protective factors as being responsible for overcoming difficult life circumstances:

Individual/Within – At age one their mothers described them as cuddly, friendly, cheerful, responsive and sociable. By age 10 the children displayed problem-solving skills, read and behaved better than those with development problems. Belief in their ability and realistic educational goals with higher future life expectations was a key element.

Family – Close bond with at least one emotionally stable person who took care of their needs. Extra nurturing from grandparents, aunts, older siblings and uncles, which all became surrogate parents. Resilient boys came from households with structure and rules through a male model of identification. Resilient girls came from families with an emphasis on independence and support from a female caregiver.

Community – Relying on elders and peers in their community for emotional support and counsel in times of crisis. Teacher role modelling, caring neighbors, youth leaders and members of other church groups.

It is interesting to note that most of the troubled youth had recovered between the ages of 32 and 40. The most important note to take from the study is that the *opening of opportunities* in the third and fourth decade of their life led to long-lasting positive change.

This shows that regardless of where you start in life, the opportunities you seek, as an adult, have a greater impact in your life.

The good news is that resilience is not a personality trait, but more of a dynamic learning process. When encountering moments of crisis, the automatic thoughts are ones of chaos.

Resilience begins by switching your thinking process to see the adversity as a learning process and a chance for personal development and growth.

One step to developing resilience is placing the individual event into a bigger context. Many of us tend to catastrophize.

TIP!
Zooming in and out of your problem is a visualization technique that has shown positive results. You begin by zooming out of the room you are in to the sky, then the moon, then the stars, then space until all you can see is the earth from far, far away.

How big is your problem now?
Resilience training is a personal journey and there are many strategies you can undertake. The strategies below are recommended by the American Psychological Association.

1. Make connections. Good relationships with close family members, friends or others are important. Accepting help and support from those who care about you strengthens resilience. Some people find activities in civic groups, or other local groups provides social support and can help them in reclaiming hope.

2. Avoid seeing crises as unsolvable problems. You can't change that stressful events happen, but you can change how you interpret and respond to these events. Try looking beyond the present to how future circumstances may be a little better.

3. Accept that change is a part of living. Certain goals may no longer be attainable because of adverse situations. Accepting circumstances that cannot be changed can help you focus on circumstances you can change.

4. Move toward your goals. Develop some realistic goals. Do something even if it seems like a small accomplishment. This enables you to move toward your goals. Ask yourself: "What's one thing I know I can accomplish today that will help me move in the direction I want to go?"

5. Take decisive actions. Act on adverse situations as much as you can. Take decisive actions rather than detaching from problems and stresses and wishing they would just go away.

6. Look for opportunities for self-discovery. People often learn something about themselves and may find they have grown in some respect because of their struggle with loss. Many people who have experienced tragedies and hardship have reported better relationships and a heightened appreciation for life.

7. Nurture a positive view of yourself. This can be done by focusing on being the best you, stop criticizing your appearance, be good to your body,

spend time with people that love you and you love. Developing confidence in your ability to solve problems and trusting your instincts helps build resilience.

8. Keep things in perspective. Even when facing very painful events, try to consider the stressful situation in a broader context and keep a long-term perspective. Avoid blowing the event out of proportion.

9. Maintain a hopeful outlook. An optimistic outlook enables you to expect that good things will happen in your life. Try visualizing what you want rather than worrying about what you fear.

10. Take care of yourself. Pay attention to your own needs and feelings. Engage in activities you enjoy and find relaxing. Exercise. Taking care of yourself helps to keep your mind and body primed to deal with situations that require resilience.

In the end, you and only you can control the interpretation of events. By enriching your resilience bank, you are better prepared for life's journey. One of my favorite quotes from the Rocky Balboa movie is:

"It's not how hard you can hit, but how hard you can get hit and get back up again." –Sylvester Stallone.

Positive psychology views resilience as the ability to cope with whatever life throws at you and return as a stronger person than ever before.

*"The greatest glory in living lies not in never falling, but in rising every time we fall." -*Nelson Mandela.

Additional notes

Resilience is more necessary than ever in our fast-paced world. The repercussions include mental burn out, fatigue and in some cases, medication.

Resilience training can be taught to youngsters at an early stage. It angers me when I see stories of people taking their own lives, due to bullying, body image issues, or social media abuse. Bullies have existed in the past and probably always will.

Part of being human is that we can't predict or control how others will behave.

However, what we can control 100% is our reaction to the events. Education and an increased awareness of resilience development methods builds a strong shield against life's hardships.

Resilience is a springboard to bring us back to a state better than before.

J.K. ROWLING

In 1994, J. K. Rowling had just got divorced, was on government aid and could barely afford to feed her baby. This was just three years before the first Harry Potter book was published. She couldn't afford a computer or even the cost of photocopying the 90,000-word novel, so she manually typed out each version to send to publishers.

Editors rejected it dozens of times until finally Bloomsbury, a London publisher, gave it a second chance after the CEO's eight-year-old, daughter fell in love with it.

"You may have to fight a battle more than once to win it."
-Margaret Thatcher.

MAKING SENSE OF IT ALL

Analyzing and digesting this material is a process. Only by putting key principles to practice can real change begin. Positive thinking is not enough in today's-society. This book is for anyone who has been thinking about positive change for a while now, but doesn't have the scientific facts and tips to help them though their journey.

For the natural-born optimists hopefully this book will remind you to be grateful more often.

For the sceptics who had the courage to pick up and flick through the pages and try out at least one or even two positive psychology practices mentioned: Well done!
For everyone else who loves life and wants to discover how to enhance their journey: Good choice!

When all is said, and done, what is life all about?
Life is a cluster of moments which define us. Family, holidays, career, possessions, all that and much more are scenes in the most spectacular theatrical play of all.

So how would you like to look back when you're in your nineties?

To a life full of missed opportunities, buts, excuses and should haves? Or a life lived to the fullest while making the most of every opportunity?

Looking back and remembering hardship and suffering, which we all experience to an extent, is a choice. Just, as focusing on moments of joy in-order to keep mentally sane and happy is a choice. We *choose* positivity not just for our own wellbeing, but for those who need us emotionally, physically, spiritually and financially. Every child wants a parent, grandparent, family member, or a friend to count on.

Positivity is for the spouse who had a hard day at work and is looking forward to coming home to a little warmth and a loving smile. It is also for the family member or friend reaching out for some positive energy when things aren't going so well.

I'm not suggesting becoming everyone's amateur therapist, especially to those clinically depressed or deeply troubled, as they need professional care. What we can all do is become a positive light that shines wherever we are and watch everyone shine along with us.

I hope the simple strategies of the book will lead you to greater joy and happiness.

REFERENCES

Acevedo, E. (2012). *Exercise psychology: understanding the mental health benefits of physical activity and the public health challenges of inactivity*. In E. Acevedo (ed.) The Oxford Handbook of Exercise Psychology (pp. 3–8). New York: Oxford University Press.

American Society for Aesthetic Plastic Surgery, (2016). https://www.surgery.org/sites/default/files/ASAPS-Stats2016.pdf

Ajzen, I. (1991). *The theory of planned behaviour*. Organizational Behavior and Human Decision Processes, 50: 179–211.

Balakrishnan, J. & Griffiths, M. (2017). *An Exploratory Study of "Selfitis" and the Development of the Selfitis Behavior Scale*. International Journal of Mental Health and Addiction, June 2018, Volume 16, Issue 3, pp 722-736.

Ball size. Funny story. *Telegulu One Comedy. http://www.teluguone.com/comedy/content/ball-size-sport-joke-661-23710.html*

Bandura, A., Ross, D., & Ross, S. A. (1961). *Transmission of aggression through imitation of aggressive models*.

Blum, K. et.al., (1996). *Reward Deficiency Syndrome*. American Scientist, Vol. 84. No 2, pp. 132-145.

Bartels, M. and Boomsa, D. (2009). *Born to be happy? The etiology of subjective well-being*. Behavioral Genetics, 39: 605–15.

Bartels, M., Saviouk, V., deMoor, M.H.M. et al. (2010). *Heritability and genome-wide linkage scan of subjective happiness*. Twin Research and Human Genetics, 13(2): 135–42.

Baumeister, R.F. and Leary, M. (1995). *The need to belong: desire for interpersonal attachments as a fundamental human motivation*.

Psychological Bulletin, 117: 497–529.

Benton, D. and Donohue, R.T. (1999). *The effect of nutrients on mood.* Public Health Nutrition, 2(3A): 403–9.

Biddle, S.J.H. and Mutrie, N. (2007). *Psychology of Physical Activity: Determinants, Well-being and Interventions.* (2nd edn). London: Routledge.

Bird on a branch (2018) – Story of confidence. *Mind fuel daily.* https://www.mindfueldaily.com/livewell/short-story-to-inspire-self-confidence/

Breuning, G. L. (2012). *Meet Your Happy Neurochemicals: Dopamine, Endorphine, Oxytocin, Serotonin.* SystemIntegrityPress.com.

Brown, K.W. and Ryan, R.M. (2003). *The benefits of being present: mindfulness and its role in psychological well-being.* Journal of Personality and Social Psychology, 84: 822–48.

Bryant, F., & Veroff, J. (2007). *Savoring: A New Model of Positive Experience.* Lawrence Erlbaum Associates, Inc., Publishers. 1o Industrial Avenue, Mahwah, New Jersey, 07430.

Byrne, R. (2006). *The Secret.* Simon & Schuster, Inc. 1230 Avenue of the Americas, New York, NY 10020.

Buckingham, M. & Cliffton, D. (2001). *Now, Discover Your Strengths.* The Free Press. A Division of Simon & Schuster Inc. 1230 Avenue of the Americas, New York. NY 10020.

Carr, A. (2011). Positive Psychology: *The Science of Happiness and Human Strengths.* (2nd edn). Hove: Brunner-Routledge.

Carter, S. (2009). *Oxytocin.* In S. Lopez (ed.) The Encyclopedia of Positive Psychology (pp. 38–40). Chichester: Blackwell Publishing Ltd.

Castle, D., Honigman, R. and Phillips, K. (2002*). Does cosmetic surgery improve psychosocial wellbeing?* Medical Journal of Australia, 176(12): 601–4.

Cattell, H. & Schuerger, J. (2003). *Essentials of 16PF Assessment (Essentials of Psychological Assessment).* John Wiley & Sons Inc. 111 River Street, Hoboken, NJ 07030.

Clifton, J. (2018). *Gallup Organization – Clifton Strengths Finder.* https://

www.gallupstrengthscenter.com/

Cohn, M. and Fredrickson, B. (2009). *Broaden-and-build theory of positive emotions.* In S. Lopez (ed.) The Encyclopedia of Positive Psychology (pp. 105–10).

Compton, W. and Hoffman, E. (2012). *Positive Psychology: The Science of Happiness and Flourishing.* (2nd edn). USA: Wadsworth Cengage Learning.

Craig, B. W. et.al. (1989). *Effects of progressive resistance training on growth hormone and testosterone levels in young and elderly subjects.* https://www.ncbi.nlm.nih.gov/pubmed/2796409

Csikszentmihalyi, M. (1975). *Beyond Boredom and Anxiety.* San Franscisco, CA: Jossey-Bass.

Csikszentmihalyi, M. (1990) Flow: *The Psychology of Optimal Experience.* New York: Harper and Row.

Csikszentmihalyi, M. and Csikszentmihalyi, I. (1988). *Optimal Experience: Psychological Studies of Flow in Consciousness.* New York: Cambridge University Press.

Deci, L. E. & Ryan, M. R. (2017). *Self-Determination Theory: Basic Psychological Needs in Motivation, Development, and Wellness.* The Guildford Press. A Division of Guildford Publications, Inc. 370 Seventh Avenue, Suite 1200, New York, NY 1001.

Danner, D., Snowdon, D. and Friesen, W. (2001). *Positive emotions in early life and longevity: findings from the Nun Study.* Journal of Personality and Social Psychology, 80(5): 804–13.

DeNeve, K. and Cooper, H. (1998). *The happy personality: a meta-analysis of 137 personality traits and subjective well-being.* Psychological Bulletin, 124: 197–229.

Diener, E. (2000). *Subjective well-being – the science of happiness and a proposal for a national index.* American Psychologist, 55(1): 34–43.

Diener, E. and Chan, M. (2011). *Happy people live longer: subjective well-being contributes to health and longevity.* Applied Psychology: Health and Well-Being, 3: 1–43.

Donaldson, D. (2001). *Subjective, Intersubjective, Objective.* Oxford University Press. Great Clarendon Street, Oxford OX2 6DP.

Dweck, C. S. (2006). *Mindset: The New Psychology of Success.* New York: Random House.

Easterling, A, R. (2010). *Happiness, Growth, and the Life Cycle.* Oxford University Press. Great Clarendon Street, Oxford, OX2 6DP, United Kingdom.

Eckman, P. and Davidson, R.J. (1993). *Voluntary smiling changes regional brain activity.* Psychological Science, 4: 342–5.

Educational Psychology in context. Readings for future teachers. SAGE Publications, Thousand Oakes, 57-66.

Emmons, R.A. and McCullough, M.E. (2003). *Counting blessings versus burdens: an experimental investigation of gratitude and subjective well-being in daily life.* Journal of Personality and Social Psychology, 84(2): 377–89.

Eriksson, N., et al. (2010). Web-based, participant driven studies yield novel genetic associations for common traits. https://journals.plos.org/plosgenetics/article?id=10.1371/journal.pgen.1000993

Finding Happiness (2017) - Story about happiness. *Motivational stories.* https://academictips.org/blogs/finding-happiness/

Fox, K. R. (2000). *Self-esteem, self-perceptions and exercise.* International Journal of Sport Psychology, 31(2): 228–40.

Fredrickson, B. (2001). *The role of positive emotions in positive psychology: the broaden-and-build theory of positive emotions.* American Psychologist, 56(3): 218–26.

Gardener, H. (2006). *Multiple Intelligences: New Horizons in Theory and Practice.* Basic Books, Perseus Books Group, USA.

Griffiths, D. M, & Balakrishnan, J. (2017). *An Explanatory Study of "Selfitis" and the Development of the Selfitis Behaviour Scale.* International Journal of Mental Health and Addiction, June 2018, Volume 16, Issue 3, pp 722-736. https://link.springer.com/article/10.1007/s11469-017-9844-x

Gross, R. (2002). *Socrate's Way: Seven Keys to Using Your Mind.* Penguin Putnam Inc. 375 Hudson Street, New York, NY 10014.

Ginis, K., Bassett, R. and Conlin, C. (2012). *Body image and exercise.* In E. Acevedo (ed.) The Oxford Handbook of Exercise Psychology (pp. 55–75). New York: Oxford University Press.

Goldberg, H. (2006). *HIPPOCRATES: Father of Medicine.* Choice Press, 2021 Pine Lake Road, Suite 100. Lincoln, NE 68512, USA.

Goldberg, L, R. (1993). *The Structure of Phenotypic Personality Traits.* American Psychologist, 48, 26-34. http://dx.doi.org/10.1037/0003-066X.48.1.26

Haidt, J. (2006). *The Happiness Hypothesis: Finding Modern Truth in Ancient Wisdom.* Basic Books, Park Avenue South, New York, NY 10016-8810.

Hanson, R. and Mendius, R. (2009). *Buddha's Brain: The Practical Neuroscience of Happiness, Love, and Wisdom.* Oakland, CA: New Harbinger Publications.

Hausenblas, H.A. and Fallon, E.A. (2006). *Relationship between exercise and body image: a meta-analysis.* Psychology and Health, 21: 33–47.

Healthy Eating, Physical Activity, Body Image and Self-Esteem Common Messages Discussion Paper May 2009 CANADA.

Heart of Gratitude (2008) – Story of blind boy. https://motivateus.com/stories/the-blind-boy.htm

Hecht, D. (2013). *The Neural Basis of Optimism and Pessimism. https://www.ncbi.nlm.nih.gov/pmc/articles/PMC3807005/*

Hefferon, K. and Mutrie, N. (2012). *Physical activity as a 'stellar' positive psychology intervention.* In E. Acevedo (ed.) Oxford Handbook of Exercise Psychology (pp. 117–30). Oxford: Oxford University Press.

Hefferon, Kate. (2013). *Positive Psychology And The Body: The Somatopsychic Side To Flourishing.* Open University Press, McGraw-Hill Education, Shoppenhangers Road, Maidenhead, Berkshire, England, SL6 2QL.

Hollander, D. and Kraemer, R. (2012). *Psychology of resistance exercise.*

In E. Acevedo (ed.) The Oxford Handbook of Exercise Psychology (pp. 465–89). New York: Oxford University Press.

Hull, C. (1943). *Principles of Behavior.* New York: Appleton-Century-Crofts.

Ivtzan, I. (2012). *Mindfulness and positive psychology.*

J.K. Rowling (2017). *Broke but not broken.* Short story. https://www.jdmindcoach.com/jk-rowling-broke-not-broken/

Kagan, J. (1998). *Galen's Prophecy: Temperament In Human Nature.* Taylor & Francis Group, 711 Third Avenue, New York, NY 10017, USA.

Kahneman, D., Diener, E. and Schwarz, N. (1999). *Well-Being: The Foundations of Hedonic Psychology.* New York: Russell Sage Foundation.

Kashdan, T.B., Biswas-Diener, R. and King, L.A. (2008). *Reconsidering happiness: The costs of distinguishing between hedonics and eudaimonia.* Journal of Positive Psychology, 3: 219–33.

Keyes, C.L.M. (2006). *Subjective well-being in mental health and human development research worldwide: an introduction.* Social Indicators Research, 77: 1–10.

Layard, A. (2006). Happiness: *Lessons from a New science.* Penguin Group, Penguin Books Ltd, 80 Strand, London WC2 ORL, England.

Linley, A. (2009). *Positive psychology (history).* In S. Lopez (ed.) The Encyclopedia of Positive Psychology (pp. 742–6). Chichester: Blackwell Publishing Ltd.

Lyken, D. & Tellegen, A. (1996). *Happiness is a Stochastic Phenomenon.* Psychological Science. Volume: 7 issue: 3 page(s): 186-189. Sage Journals. https://doi.org/10.1111/j.1467-9280.1996.tb00355.x

Lyubomirsky, S., King, L.A. and Diener, E. (2005). *The benefits of frequent positive affect: does happiness lead to success?* Psychological Bulletin, 131: 803–55.

Marston, M, W. (2008*). Emotions of Normal People.* New York, Harcourt, Brace and Company, 1928.

Maslow, H. A. (1943). *A theory of human motivation.* Sublime Books, PO Box 632, Floyd, VA 24091-0632, (2014).

McRae, R, R. & Costa, T, P. (2003). *Personality in Adulthood: A Five-Factor Theory Perspective.* A Division of Guildford Publications, Inc. 72 Spring Street, New York, NY 10012.

Money can't buy happiness (2016) - Story – *fiction. https://steemit.com/life/@giantbear/money-can-t-buy-happiness-an-original-story-fiction*

Myers, B, I, & Myers, B, P. (1980). *Gifts Differing: Understanding Personality Type.* Davies-Black Publishing, a division of CPP, Inc., 1055 Joaquin Road, 2ⁿᵈ Floor, Mountain View, CA 94043.

Park, N., Peterson, C. and Seligman, M. (2004). *Strengths of character and well-being.* Journal of Social and Clinical Psychology, 23: 603–19.

Peterson, C. and Seligman, M. (2004). *Character Strengths and Virtues: A Handbook and Classification.* New York: Oxford University Press.

Robins, T. (1991). *Awaken the Giant Within.* Free Press. A division of Simon & Shuster, Inc. 1230 Avenue of the Americas New York, New York 10020.

Rhodes, R. and Pfaeffli, L. (2012). *Personality and physical activity.* In E. Acevedo (ed.) The Oxford Handbook of Exercise Psychology (pp. 195–223). New York: Oxford University Press.

Ryff, C.D. and Keyes, C.L.M. (1995). *The structure of psychological well-being revisited.* Journal of Personality and Social Psychology, 69(4): 719–27.

Saphire-Bernstein, S., Way, B.M., Kim, H.S., Sherman, D.K. and Taylor, S.E. (2011). *Oxytocin receptor gene 360 (OXTR) is related to psychological resources.* Proceedings of the National Academy of Sciences, 108(15): 118–22.

Scheier, M. and Carver, C. (2009). *Optimism.* In S. Lopez (ed.) The Encyclopedia of Positive Psychology (pp. 656–63). Chichester: Blackwell Publishing Ltd.

Shamay –Tsoory, S. et.al. (2009). *Intranasal administration of oxytocin increases envy and schadenfreude (gloating). https://www.ncbi.nlm.nih.gov/pubmed/19640508*

Shapiro D. A, & Shapiro, D. (1982). *Meta-analysis of comparative therapy outcome studies: A replication and refinement.* Psychological Bulletin, Vol

92(3):581-604. http://psycnet.apa.org/buy/1983-06160-001

Seligman, M. (2002). *Authentic Happiness: Using the New Positive Psychology to Realize Your Potential for Lasting Fulfilment.* New York: Free Press.

Seligman, M. (2006). *Learned Optimism: How to change your mind and life.* New York: Vintage Books.

Seligman, M. (2007). *Positive Psychology, Positive Prevention, and Positive Therapy.* https://www.sas.upenn.edu/psych/seligman/ppsnyderchapter. htm

Seligman, M. (2011). *Flourish.* Free Press. A Division of Simon & Shuster, Inc. 1230 Avenue of the Americas, New York, NY 10020.

Tali, S. (2011). *The Optimism Bias.* Pantheon Books, a division of Random House, Inc. New York.

Taylor, S. (2012). *Health Psychology* (8th edn). Los Angeles, CA: McGraw-Hill Education.

Tellegen, A., Lykken, D.T., Bouchard, T.J. et al. (1988). *Personality similarity in twins reared apart and together.* Journal of Personality and Social Psychology, 54: 1031–9.

The Belly and the Members (2015) – Story about positive bodies. https://www.bartleby.com/17/1/29.html

The Boy Who Harnessed the Wind (2009) – Story of passion and possibility. https://www.brainpickings.org/2012/01/26/the-boy-who-harnessed-the-wind-zinon/

The Pleasure of Freedom (2018) – Story of pleasure. http://www.english-for-students.com/The-Pleasure-of-Freedom.html

The Two Travelers (2010) – Story about optimism. *Inspirational stories.* https://betterlifecoachingblog.com/2010/07/30/the-two-travellers-a-story-about-optimism/

The Wise Man (2018) – Short story of moral lessons. https://www.wattpad.com/492149757-short-stories-with-moral-lessons-the-wise-man

Tiberius, V. and Hall, A. (2010). *Normative theory and psychological research: hedonism, eudaimonism, and why it matters.* Journal of Positive Psychology, 5(3): 212–25.

Value (2008) – Short inspirational story. http://www.inspirationpeak.com/cgi-bin/stories.cgi?record=33

Vaillant, G., et al., (2010). *Grant Study of Adult Development, 1938-2000. https://dataverse.harvard.edu/dataset.xhtml?persistentId=hdl:1902.1/00290*

Vallerand, R. J. (2015). *The Psychology of Passion: A Dualistic Model.* Oxford University Press, 198 Madison Avenue, New York, NY 10016.

Vincent, J. (2014). American Psychiatric Association makes it official: *'Selfie' is a mental disorder.* Adobo Chronicles, March 31. https://adobochronicles.com/2014/03/31/american-psychiatric-association-makes-it-official-selfie-a-mental-disorder/

Waterman, A. S. (1993). *Two Conceptions of Happiness: Contrasts of Personal Expressiveness (Eudaimonia) and Hedonic Enjoyment.* Journal of Personality and Social Psychology, 64, 678-691.

Waterman, A. S. (1995). *Eudaimonic theory: Self-realization and the collective good.* In W. M. Kurtines & J. L. Gewirtz (Eds.), *Moral development: An introduction.* (p. 255-278). Boston: Allyn & Bacon.

Weiss, A., Bates, T.C. and Luciano, M. (2008). *Happiness is a personal(ity) thing: The genetics of personality and well-being in a representative sample.* Psychological Science, 19: 205–9.

Werner, E. E. and Smith, R. S. (2001) *Journeys from Childhood to Midlife: Risk, Resilience, and Recovery* by Emmy E. Werner and Ruth S. Smith. New York, NY: Cornell University Press.

World Happiness Report, (2017). http://worldhappiness.report/ed/2017/

Wundt, W. (1912). *An Introduction to Psychology.* George Allen & Unwin, ltd. Ruskin House, 40 Museum St. WC1.

Yerkes, R. M. & Dodson, J. D. (1908). *The Relation of Strength of Stimulus to Rapidity of Habit-Formation.* Journal of Comparative Neurology and Psychology,18, 459-482.

NOTES: